Renaissance Architecture in Venice 1450-1540

Renaissance Architecture in Venice 1450-1540

Ralph Lieberman

Frederick Muller Limited
London

In memoriam Kirkland College 1965–1978

First published in Great Britain in 1982 by
Frederick Muller Limited, London SW19 7JZ

© 1982 John Calmann and Cooper Ltd, London

This book was designed and produced by
John Calmann and Cooper Ltd, London
Designer: Gail Engert

ISBN 0-584-95034-9

Typeset in Great Britain by SX Composing Ltd, Rayleigh
Printed in Italy

Frontispiece View of Venice from the bell-tower of
San Giorgio Maggiore

Contents

San Fantino. Nave, begun *c.* 1507

Preface

'Renaissance' is an unclear word, in part because writers use it as both a chronological and a stylistic designation. In the first case it is usually redundant, and in the second case frequently restricting. If it means only a period, it is no more informative than dates. If it means primarily or solely a classicizing style, it is almost never universally applicable, even to as short a span as a decade. This is particularly the case with Venetian architecture between about 1450 and 1530, when the Classical was only one of several currents, including the late Gothic and the Byzantine revival, to be observed in the buildings, and when works in widely varying architectural styles were often produced at the same time, occasionally by the same architect. Different styles were not always viewed as mutually exclusive, or even as necessarily reflecting opposing attitudes and intentions.

The richly varied buildings of this period are not without unity, however, but it is to be found in their experimental and exploratory approach to architecture rather than in a clear, dominant style.

If we consider the Classical revival in terms of its character rather than its style, we find that it was motivated by a new historical consciousness and resulted from a search through ancient architecture for authoritative forms. The Byzantine revival of late 15th-century Venice, while very different in style from the Classical revival, reveals an analogous point of view and a similar use of the past. In this book, then, 'Early Renaissance' refers neither to a period nor to a specific style, but to an attitude toward the past, and to the active, sometimes restless search for a new expressive mode which dominated Venetian architecture from the 1450s to the 1530s.

Beginning around 1450 we see a quickening of the rate of architectural change, and a transformation of its character. A wider range of architectural sources and traditions was reconsidered in the buildings of the next eighty years than in the preceding two centuries. My goal in this presentation is to define and describe this new approach, as well as to distinguish it from the one that began to replace it in the 1530s, when we first find a more insistent and severe Classical style and a more certain, less experimental attitude that must be seen as fundamentally different from the Early Renaissance spirit.

Architecture is studied out of context at the risk of misunderstanding it, and in the Introduction I have therefore tried to present the cultural, historical and social background against which the buildings ought to be seen. I have considered questions of architectural practice also, for the technical, administrative and commercial aspects of construction strongly impinge on the study of Venetian architecture.

In the following sections the buildings are organized according to type: churches, family chapels, palace façades, *scuole* and civic buildings. While this small book cannot include every building constructed in Venice during the period it covers, it does offer a full indication of the architectural range of the epoch. In presenting a complex period in its broad outlines I have had to simplify things at times, but have not done so excessively and, if this book is not exhaustive, it nevertheless provides a broad view of all the major tendencies and some of the minor ones in Venetian building of the late 15th and early 16th centuries.

Venice is loved and visited by many people, but with a few important exceptions her architecture is relatively unstudied. This book is intended primarily to present to the reader a historically important period and many beautiful buildings he or she may not have known before. In view of the physical deterioration of much Venetian architecture, and the growing concern that it is disappearing before our eyes, this book should also help people recognize what is unique about the threatened works, and appreciate the scale of the potential loss.

All of the photographs presented here are new and unpublished; they were taken by the author especially for this book. New photographs of old buildings are necessary not only to show their present condition and use or re-use, but because every photograph, of any period, freezes into a single mood a building which, through changes of light and season, has many. These new pictures are not intended to replace the old views but to augment them, and to widen the experience of those who have not seen the buildings *in situ*.

A map of Venice is included (see p. 31) to help the reader establish the general location in the city of all the buildings discussed in the book.

To those who plan to visit Venice, or who may be there while reading this book, I repeat an old counsel. In *The Stones of Venice*, when advising the traveller looking at buildings in the city, John Ruskin wrote that he 'would ask him to stay his gondola beside each of them long enough to examine their every line'. Few of us nowadays can afford the luxury of studying architecture from a gondola, but Ruskin's urging that the visitor look with care is perpetually apt. This book is intended as an aid to that looking, not as a substitute for it. My efforts will be repaid when the reader notices aspects of the buildings I have not mentioned, and discovers connections and relationships that I have overlooked.

Acknowledgments

I wish to thank Signorina Lorenza Mattiazzo of Venice for her constant care and attention in the developing and printing of my photographs. Without her help my work would have been much more difficult.

To Edith Foster I owe many thanks for years of thought-provoking conversations about architecture in Venice. To all the members of the Lanfranchi family I am deeply grateful for hospitality and friendship over a period of many years.

To the Samuel H. Kress Foundation I am much indebted for the timely assistance that enabled me to return to Venice in the summer of 1978 so that I could write about Venetian architecture in the presence of the buildings themselves.

Palazzo Ducale. Scala dei Giganti, begun
c. 1485. Antonio Rizzo

Introduction

For those who like their art history simple and straightforward the study of Venetian architecture between about 1450 and 1540 is a tribulation. Rather than clear lines of development and apparently inevitable changes, there seem only false starts and retrogressions. The often self-conscious variety that characterizes the era resulted from the influence of several traditions. These were the Gothic, which survived into the 16th century; the ancient Roman, with its very different forms, system and associations; the 15th-century Romanesque revival and Classical revival styles of Brunelleschi and Alberti; and the very strong local Byzantine tradition. These did not exert their influence uniformly. Within each building type there are tendencies not apparent in the others; palaces and *scuole* developed differently from churches of the same period.

It is the historian's task not simply to describe and categorize these different traditions, but to attempt to understand how and why they came to be present in a particular combination at a given place and time. With things Venetian it is always best to begin by considering the city's geographical position, for it was of fundamental importance.

Near the northern end of the Adriatic, Venice lay between the Latin-Germanic west and the Byzantine east. Perhaps because she was situated exactly at the edge of two cultures, Venice was at once estranged from and drawn to each, sometimes exhibiting signs of these reactions simultaneously.

Venice was never a Roman city; the lagoon was not extensively settled before the 6th century, the city not established in its present location until the 9th. While myth had it that the first Venetians were Roman refugees from the mainland who fled into the lagoon to escape barbarian invaders, the city's post-Classical foundation and Byzantine associations contributed to a strong sense of separation from Italy, and she always refused to accept the fiction of the authority and imperial continuity of the Holy Roman Empire.

The Venetian connection with the East was similarly inconsistent. The upper Adriatic coast was under Byzantine control by the 5th century, and Venice was still regarded, by the Byzan-tines at least, as part of their empire in the early 9th century. But she was located very far from the Byzantine capital at Constantinople and, as Eastern power in the Adriatic declined, the Emperor exerted less and less political authority. As early as the 9th century, when she had to steer a delicate course between the Franks and the Byzantines, Venice revealed her characteristic policy of balancing East and West, often managing to extract advantageous trade agreements from both sides.

The Western and Byzantine legacies came together in an interesting way in the mid-15th century, when Venetians began to regard themselves, and even to be regarded by foreigners, as 'new Romans'. While this label was intended primarily to express Venetian military power and political stability, there is a multiple meaning in it. Constantinople, the capital of the Eastern Empire, had been founded in Byzantium in the 4th century as New Rome. The Venetians' self-description suggests that they saw themselves as the heirs to the Eastern Empire, which fell to the Ottoman Turks in 1453, as well as to the Western; they were both new Romans and New Romans.

On a north-south line medieval Europe was divided between the domains of the Holy Roman Emperor and the Pope. While Venice lay in the area of northern Italy claimed by the Emperor in the 12th century she managed, by virtue of her maritime position on the Adriatic coast, to keep herself separate and free from Imperial authority. At the same time she studiously avoided too close an association with the Pope and anti-Imperial factions. In 1177, as the culmination of her policy of careful detachment, she brought Pope Alexander III and Emperor Frederick Barbarossa together to reconcile their differences in the Truce of Venice. It was one of the city's proudest moments, and did much to establish her self-image as independent, yet indispensable to everyone.

Venice's fine and naturally protected port and her perfectly central location guaranteed the constant trade which established the city as a major conduit for goods and ideas moving both north-south and east-west. This ultimately resulted in the combination of widely varying sources which gave Venice her special cultural character. In a city with no natural resources save salt and fish, but with the means to accommodate vast trade, everything could be, and was, imported. From the beginning of her history Venice was always willing to import or to expropriate what she did not have. This was the case not only with timber from the mainland and stone from Istria, the materials with which the city was built, but with her culture, and to some extent with her identity as well. As a city which had not existed at the time of the apostles or the formation of the early Church, Venice felt herself at a disadvantage as she began to emerge as a major personality in the Christian world, so in the early 9th century two Venetian adventurers stole the body of St Mark from Alexandria and brought it to Venice, where he was made the patron saint of the city. A story was then invented to the effect that St Mark had been told by Christ that one day he would rule over the lagoon, and the theft was justified as Venetian intervention to fulfil the promise.

In later periods the Venetians revealed that they were still perfectly content to import ideas and make them their own. This may be seen clearly in the architecture of the city during the second half of the 15th century, but that is not the only medium in which her mixed cultural parentage is to be observed, nor was it by any means the earliest. Venetian property laws of the 12th and 13th centuries show combinations of Greco-Byzantine and Roman traditions that are eloquent testimony to the varied inheritance of the city. The Venetian dialect too is a microcosm of the city's culture, combining Greek, Latin, Italian, Spanish and Arabic words into a superbly expressive and idiosyncratic whole.

By the mid-15th century Venice had been a major European crossroads for five hundred years. Because of her location and cosmopolitan character, the city quickly became, in exactly the years we are considering, a major centre of the book industry. The first printing press was established in Venice in 1469, and by the century's end there were nearly two hundred, drawing scholars from all over Europe and the East.

The Venetian heritage of many cultural traditions and ideas prohibited a single style from dominating the architecture of the city in the 15th century. Nevertheless, many students of 15th-century Italian architecture have looked for the first 'Renaissance' building in Venice. To this impossible title there has been a succession of rival claimants, including the portal of the Arsenale, the city's navy yard (Plate 70), the portal of Ss.

Giovanni e Paolo (Plate 2), and the uncompleted Cà del Duca (Plate 57). None of these is completely satisfying as the herald of a new architectural style, for each represents only one thread in a complex weave. It is the variety of architectural expression that is the new element, and these three stylistically diverse works reflect it.

The buildings just mentioned have one important thing in common: all date from the late 1450s. Around the middle of the 15th century something began to change in Venetian architecture; we find a new awareness of the variety of traditions that could actively be drawn upon, and an unprecedented concern for the creation of a local Venetian style that would be an amalgam of the many elements of the city's architectural heritage.

The new breadth of style in the 1450s is revealed clearly by

Fig. 1 Pula, Yugoslavia: Arch of the Sergii, c. 30 BC

the contrast between the ground storey of the San Zaccaria façade (Fig. 2; Plate 8) and the Arsenale portal (Plate 70). Both works are generally attributed to Antonio Gambello; the first on documentary evidence, the second on the basis of long tradition. The Arsenale portal, which bears the inscribed date 1460, is the first example of architecture in Venice to show a clear and unmistakable Classical source; the lower section was derived from the Arch of the Sergii (Fig. 1) in Pula, a town on the Istrian peninsula (now Yugoslavia), where much of the stone for Venetian buildings was quarried.

The lower storey of the San Zaccaria façade descends from a different tradition; the small, twisted colonnettes attached to the edges of the façade buttresses, both in their scale and placement, maintain a Venetian style of corner treatment that can be observed in the Cà d'Oro (Fig. 15) and many other 14th- and early 15th-century palace façades. The patterned inlay of red and white marble reflects a clear Venetian fondness for polychrome effects. Given the fact that the Arsenale portal looks to an antique monument and the San Zaccaria façade ground storey to a more recent Gothic past, we might for a moment be tempted to think that the former shows a new energetic and experimental classicism while the latter represents a routine Gothicism. All such easy assumptions are, however, useless. The treatment of the San Zaccaria façade is in fact unprecedented; we know of no other church façade of the preceding two hundred years that was decorated in this rich manner, and the sources for such a treatment, rather than being clearly in the local ecclesiastical mainstream, are unknown. While the richly encrusted style of the San Zaccaria façade is small-scale and Gothic in character, the architect was experimenting intelligently with the traditional elements and drawing as well on a treasury of forms from domestic architecture, rather than passively repeating any established pattern. On the other hand, the suggestion that the Arsenale indicates the emergence of a new architectural style based on antique forms is inaccurate, for no later 15th-century work was to be as antique in style or as clearly based on an ancient Roman model. Despite what appears to be a promising start, the Venetians did not develop a strongly Roman-derived architecture in the second half of the 15th century. The Arsenale portal was a unique solution to the particular problem of creating a major entrance to a state military installation. A Roman triumphal arch found in Venetian territory was regarded as an appropriate model for it. In the same years, then, one architect could very

closely copy a Roman arch and invent a completely new type of Gothic façade decoration by fusing a variety of traditions.

It is important to note that while the Arch of the Sergii was well known to Venetian architects, they did not begin by copying it, as one might have expected, but absorbed its influences gradually before advancing to a fairly exact copy. The portals of the Madonna dell'Orto (Plate 1) and Ss. Giovanni e Paolo (Plate 2), show a development that seems to lead to the Arsenale portal. This step-by-step approximation of a model is something that we will observe in the development of church plans in the 1490s, and in that case too the period of very close copying was brief, no more than a few years.

If the Arsenale portal was largely without influence as an antique Roman revival, there was nevertheless a classicizing

Fig. 2 San Zaccaria. Ground storey of the façade, begun 1458. Antonio Gambello

force at work in Venice, although it did not always manifest itself in Classical forms.

Architecture is a language, and as such can be thought to consist of two fundamental elements: vocabulary and syntax. By vocabulary is meant primarily the style of the forms: a capital, a moulding or a columnar proportion can be based on the types and ratios of ancient Roman architecture, or on Romanesque or Gothic models. By syntax is meant the way these elements are combined. A building with Classical vocabulary may exhibit its forms in sequences, combinations and proportions that are quite the opposite of the spirit of antique architecture. Or a building in which the elements themselves are Gothic may reveal a concern for symmetry, proportion and consistency of scale that we associate with Classical architecture. The façades of the Cà d'Oro (Fig. 15), built in the second quarter of the 15th century, and the Palazzo dell'Ambasciatore (Plate 13), built in the third quarter, are very different. The asymmetry, the lack of alignment of the vertical elements, and the dense, rich elaboration of the carved surfaces of the Cà d'Oro are gone in the later building where, although there are virtually no Classical elements on the façade, there is a sense of balance, order, and subdued elegance that is Classical in spirit. On the other hand, at the Cà Dario (Plate 16), built in the late 1480s, the capitals, pilasters and mouldings are mostly Classical but, apart from the lowest storey which is symmetrically arranged around the water-gate, the building shows a pronounced asymmetry in the distribution of windows, balconies and decorative devices. Here Classical details are utilized in a very un-Classical arrangement, one that in fact rather closely resembles the Cà d'Oro. The Palazzo dell'Ambasciatore and the Cà Dario are not easy to classify stylistically. We can find one set of criteria for concluding that one is still Gothic, the other Classical, and another set for exactly the opposite conclusion. The decision will depend on whether we concentrate on their forms or their organization, on their vocabulary or their syntax.

The difficulties in describing the style of 15th-century Venetian buildings are paralleled by the difficulties in dating them. In the absence of documentary or archaeological evidence the only basis for dating a building is its style, but in Venice this is often an unreliable indicator, for buildings of quite different styles are documented to the same years; we have seen that individual architects sometimes worked in two different styles at once. As a result, dates of Venetian buildings are often debated,

and the ones offered here may not always be in accord with those suggested by other students of the field.

The study of Venetian architecture is further complicated when we come to deal with the architects themselves. If we mean by 'architect' a person who functioned exclusively as the designer of buildings, almost no one would meet the description; in this period there was no such thing as an architectural profession.

We are not as well informed as we would like to be about the varied activities of men who built buildings in Venice. Virtually all of them were trained as stonecutters and a number of them as sculptors; they came to the building profession through a knowledge of its materials. These included wood, and on occasion a talented carpenter was called upon to execute a building in stone; in the documents relating to the spiral staircase at the Palazzo Minelli (Plate 55), the man responsible for constructing it is referred to as 'Giovanni Candi, carpenter'. This was exceptional, however, for almost all builders are referred to as masons.

Because much work was done by men trained as stonecutters and sculptors, there are some works in which the distinction between architecture and sculpture is not easy to make. This is true not only with such traditionally ambiguous forms as tombs and altarpiece frames, but with larger works such as the choir-screen of Santa Maria Gloriosa dei Frari (Plate 20). There are also some unexpected combinations of architecture and sculpture, such as the portal of Sant'Elena (Plate 27).

The appeal of a building was thought by many people in 15th-century Venice to lie more in its well-carved details than in abstract proportion or theoretical harmony (see Plate 62). The person who executed a building seems to have been considered more important than the creator of its design, and a stonecutter who could carve a graceful moulding and run an efficient shop was highly regarded. At times there seems to have been little or no hesitation in entrusting the 'design' of a building to a man who had shown himself to be a first-rate stonecutter.

When we speak of 'designs' in this period we must be very careful. There is no evidence that a set of detailed drawings was ever handed to a building crew, as it would be today. Even if drawings or wooden models were made, the details of mouldings and capitals were almost certainly not specified; they would have been left to the master to carve or delegate on the site. In the documents for many projects there is no mention of a specific designer, only the master mason and, as a result, epoch-making ideas are often anonymous. The double-ramp staircase at the Scuola San Marco, for example, which Mauro Codussi built, was part of the design well before he arrived on the scene. Perhaps even the façade (Plate 66), begun by Pietro Lombardo and Giovanni Buora and completed by Codussi, had been designed before any of them went to work on the project.

Because of the close connection between stonecutting and construction, good masons who had some business and administrative skills often worked as building supervisors or contractors; in several cases men who are known to have provided designs for buildings appear at a later date as contractors or construction supervisors on other buildings they did not design. A misunderstanding of this fact has sometimes led students to assume that whenever a man who is known to have designed buildings appears as the *proto*, or master-builder, of a project, he must have had a hand in its design. There is no support for such an assumption, and some very strong evidence to the contrary. For example, although Giorgio Spavento was paid in 1506 for the design of San Salvatore (Fig. 13; Plate 42), in 1507 the construction was contracted to Pietro Lombardo, who is referred to in the documents as the *proto*. Pietro's responsibility at San Salvatore was to see to the construction of the building, and to supervise the carving of mouldings and capitals. He was not the architect in the sense in which we use the word. Even the appointment to the office of *proto* of the Procurators of San Marco did not mean that the holder was the designer of all the architectural projects for which the Procurators were responsible; very often the *proto* simply built for the Procurators what other people had designed.

Some of the men who were at times designers and contractors were also in the stone business, and on occasion appear only as suppliers of materials. Pietro Lombardo was surely engaged in this enterprise, and on more than one occasion was commissioned to acquire stone for building projects to the design of which he had not contributed. In 1503, for example, when the decision was made to widen the Clock Tower in Piazza San Marco (Plate 74), he was given the task of procuring the best stone available.

Even if they were not in the stone business, master-masons were expected to know a good deal about stone and look to its acquisition on behalf of their patrons. On some projects, such as San Zaccaria, the position of *proto* carried with it the obligation to travel regularly to quarries in Istria and Verona to select the best available materials.

There is not as much information as we would like about the nature of architectural contracts in the later 15th century. There are a number of projects on which the *proto* changed, sometimes more than once, and there are instances in which several *proti* worked on one project. The most perplexing case is the Scuola San Marco. It burned down in 1485, and by 1489 Pietro Lombardo and Buora were under contract as *proti* of the reconstruction. Late in 1490 Antonio Rizzo and Codussi were asked to evaluate the work that had been completed to that point. From then on Pietro Lombardo and Buora no longer appear in the documents, and Codussi is named as the *proto*. Why the two men were replaced is unknown; perhaps it was an economizing measure. The Scuola was very hard pressed for money, and economized on salaries whenever possible; in 1495, before work on the Scuola was complete, Codussi himself was relieved of his permanent position as *proto* when the post was eliminated to save the monthly salary. Perhaps Pietro and Buora had a contract for a limited period, or perhaps other obligations forced them to abandon the project, as happened in other cases. It is unlikely that they were replaced out of dissatisfaction with their work, for both were well regarded, and Pietro in particular was known as honest, diligent and very responsible.

It has recently been suggested that Pietro and Buora were replaced because there had been a shift in taste toward the style of Codussi in these years, and that he offered an alternative to their largely decorative style. This brings us to the heart of the most confusing aspect of the problem; although the change is clearly known from the documents, it is not always clear who executed some parts of the building. This is the case not only at the Scuola San Marco, but in several other similar situations as well, for changes of *proto* are not always accompanied by dramatic changes in style. While commissions may sometimes have offered architects the chance to express their own ideas, often they must have consisted largely of supervising a shop already at work, and seeing to it that everything was finished properly. This is not to suggest that a new *proto* could never make his own radical or even clearly discernible contribution to a project already begun, but it is probably a mistake to assume that he would automatically have done so.

The final factor to be considered in this brief view of the Venetian building trades of the late 15th and early 16th centuries is that among the major architects, who included Bartolomeo Buon, Antonio Gambello, Mauro Codussi, Pietro Lombardo, Antonio Rizzo, Antonio Scarpagnino, Bartolomeo Bono and Jacopo Sansovino, almost none was Venetian. Gambello is the only one who belonged to a Venetian family; Buon was born in Venice but his father, a sculptor and architect, had come from Lombardy in the late 14th century. The majority of the non-Venetians were Lombards; the exceptions are Rizzo, who was born in Verona, and Sansovino, who was a Tuscan.

Not only were the important masters non-Venetian, but an army of lesser stonecutters were as well; in 1491 the Venetian stonecutters complained to the city government that it was impossible for them, tax-paying citizens of the Republic, to find work in Venice because of the number of Lombards in the city, and that these foreigners, who outnumbered them three to one, would not teach Venetians the fashionable style of architectural decoration.

It is therefore remarkable that the buildings of the city retained a clear Venetian character. While some elements of architectural decoration may be attributable to non-Venetian traditions, for the most part the city imposed its personality on the work produced there. The Venetians felt their traditions very strongly, which limited the degree to which an individual architect could depart from precedent. Only at the very end of our period was it possible for an architect to alter emphatically the style of architecture in the city. We shall see that this signals the end of the Early Renaissance.

Churches

There were three distinct phases of church building between the 1450s and the 1520s. The first was one of wide stylistic variety and experimentation with Gothic, Classical and some Byzantine elements. This was followed by the more coherent Byzantine revival phase, which in turn gave way to a phase which saw the elaboration of the Byzantine revival by its fusion with ideas from antique architecture and from the 15th- and early 16th-century Classical revival styles of Florence and Rome.

The first important work in our period took place at San Zaccaria, where Gambello began a new church in 1458 (Figs. 2–4; Plates 3, 6–8). Gambello died in 1481, before the church was finished. The nave of San Zaccaria is fairly simple (Fig. 3;

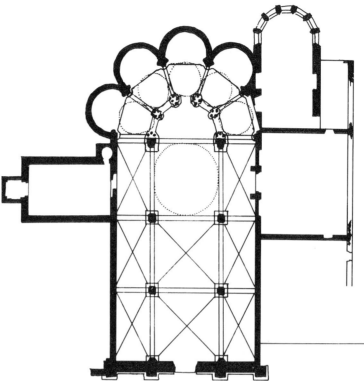

Fig. 3 San Zaccaria. Plan (after Pietro Paoletti, *L'architettura e la scultura del rinascimento in Venezia*, 1893)

Plate 3). The plan of the choir, with its unusual ambulatory and radiating chapels (Fig. 3; Plate 6), is sometimes attributed to Codussi, who took over the project in 1483. There is no documentary evidence of the replacement of an earlier choir, and it is unlikely that the church would have been under construction for twenty-five years without its liturgical nucleus organized in some way; hence credit for at least the plan of the entire church should be given to Gambello.

Aside from San Zaccaria, ambulatories are unknown in Venice, and are rare in Italy in general. The form is ultimately French in origin, but in the case of San Zaccaria there is a distinct possibility that the ambulatory derives from the 12th-century Crusader church on the site of the Holy Sepulchre in Jerusalem. The appearance of an ambulatory at San Zaccaria indicates clearly the Venetian tendency to draw on a wide variety of architectural sources and traditions. This is seen also in the contrast between the plan of the church and the details, particularly the bizarre pedestals of the nave (Fig. 4), which are fantasies on Classical decorative elements with no stylistic connection at all to the plan of the choir and ambulatory.

Codussi, who was to complete San Zaccaria after Gambello's

death, first appeared in Venice at San Michele in Isola (Plates 4, 15, 17). He began the new Camaldolese abbey church around 1468; the façade, the most striking and original part of the building, was finished by 1478. While most Venetian churches of the time had brick façades with Istrian stone or marble portals and decorative details, the San Michele façade is entirely of Istrian stone. It has an unexpected combination of elements, and its stylistic sources have long been debated. It can be regarded as an importation of Albertian ideas into Venice from Santa Maria Novella in Florence and San Francesco in Rimini (Fig. 5), or else as the development, in Renaissance vocabulary, of a façade shape already known in Venetian territory and in Venice itself before the arrival of Codussi, such as those of the Cathedral of Muggia (Plate 10) and San Giovanni in Bragora (Plate 11). Variations of the basic façade type are found in other buildings of the 1480s and 1490s (Plates 33, 66).

One revolutionary effect of the use of Istrian stone for the entire façade is that white becomes so powerful as a colour that it lends as much force to the design as the architectural elements. It is interesting to record here that white is also an important colour in Venetian painting; in the works of Giovanni Bellini, and particularly in those of Giorgione and Titian, whites are often strong and richly modulated. While it may be too much to declare that painters' sensibility to the varied possibilities of white was induced by the experience of Istrian stone architecture it is the case that in both architecture and painting there is evidence of a characteristic fondness for powerful whites.

The most striking feature of the San Michele façade is the system of strongly marked Istrian stone blocks with recessed joins. This is completely unknown in church façades in Venice or anywhere else, but it is found slightly earlier on the basement of the Cà del Duca (Plate 57). The continuation of the stone-work pattern across the pilasters is unusual even for palace façades. This is known only in Bernardo Rossellino's design for the façade of the Palazzo Piccolomini in Pienza (Fig. 6), itself derived from Alberti's Palazzo Rucellai in Florence. The influence of the Palazzo Piccolomini, which dates from the early 1460s, and the Albertian character of the San Michele façade, would suggest that Codussi had some experience in Tuscany just before he appeared in Venice, but there is no corroborating documentation for this idea.

Fig. 6 Pienza: Palazzo Piccolomini. Façade, begun 1460. Bernardo Rossellino

Fig. 7 Florence: Baptistery, begun c. 1059

Codussi's extremely original treatment of the San Michele façade, despite its close parallel with the Pienza palace, may have part of its inspiration closer to home, in Gambello's ground storey of the San Zaccaria façade (Fig. 2; Plate 8). The style of this decorative system does not resemble that of San Michele, but in each case a pattern of strongly marked rectangles continues across both wall and projections; Codussi's façade might thus be linked to an earlier Venetian work.

In the upper part of the San Michele façade Codussi tried to work a Classical system into harmony with a Gothic lobed façade. The join of the quadrant arch cornices with the pilasters of the central field is slightly awkward. The problem of how to deal with such a join was never solved and after several attempts the idea was abandoned (Plate 45).

In his first Venetian work Codussi introduced himself as a man with a much broader view of acceptable architectural combinations than most. The San Michele façade mixes local and imported, secular and religious architectural traditions of several kinds with new ideas about building materials and a fascination with Classical systems and vocabulary. What distinguishes Codussi from his predecessors is that while Gambello, for example, juxtaposed a number of contrasting styles at San Zaccaria, Codussi shows a determination to synthesize new forms from older elements.

We see this in Codussi's other early works. Although Venetian bell towers were traditionally brick, the one at San Pietro di Castello (Plates 5, 19), built by Codussi between 1482 and 1488, is Istrian stone, and has a consistent system of Classical articulation in striking contrast to other towers in the city.

The Gothic was still strong in church architecture late into the 15th century (Plates 11, 14); even into the 16th century some architects were still attempting to combine Gothic and Classical elements, as may be seen in the choir and aisle apses of Santa Maria dei Carmini (Plates 21, 22). In other cases the Gothic and new Classical style of the late 15th century were strongly juxtaposed rather than fused, as at the church of San Giacomo dell'Orio, where a new choir seems to have been designed for maximum contrast with the older nave (Plate 23).

Traditions other than the Gothic played important roles as well. At Santa Maria dei Miracoli (Plates 12, 28, 29), begun in 1481, an effort was made to utilize the exterior decorative system of the Florentine Baptistery (Fig. 7). As early as the 1460s there were interesting attempts to employ some elements of the

local Byzantine style; in the chancel of San Giobbe (Plate 25), the base of the dome is pierced with windows, as at San Marco.

In the 1460s we begin to find a new church plan, the rectangular aisle-less church, which exists in two variations. One has only a high-altar chapel, which can be either raised, as at Santa Maria dei Miracoli (Plates 28, 29), or at ground level. The second type has a ground-level high-altar chapel flanked by two smaller chapels. This type is already apparent at San Giobbe (Plates 24, 25), but is clearer at the churches of San Rocco (Plate 32) and San Sebastiano (Plate 34).

Perhaps the most interesting church architecture before the Byzantine revival of the 1490s is to be found in the parts of San Zaccaria for which Codussi was responsible. When he took over as *proto* in 1483 the church was well under way. There is no indication in the church documents that he ever tore anything down to rebuild in his own style or taste. He adapted his ideas to the parts of the building already completed or well advanced.

The three-bay nave (Plate 3), flanked by aisles, is groin-vaulted over the first two bays, but over the third is an elliptical dome (Fig. 3). The choir is much lower than the nave (Plate 6), and the aisles are continued as an ambulatory (Plate 7) behind a two-storey arcade which supports a half dome. The original design for the ambulatory probably called for groin or rib vaults to continue the pattern of the aisles around the choir, but this was changed to elliptical domes on pendentives. Like the replacement of the groin vault in the last bay of the nave, this change is attributable to Codussi on the basis of his interest in domes in several later works. The ring of domes over the ambulatory indicates that Codussi had begun to explore the possibilities of Byzantine domed sequences, but here he put the domes in a very non-Byzantine arrangement and context, bringing together in one place almost all of the styles current in the later 15th century. Codussi probably inherited the combination of Gothic and Classical forms in the choir arcade, but his addition to it of a Byzantine element was a remarkable effort to fuse a still broader range of stylistic traditions into a coherent whole. There was to be nothing like the choir of San Zaccaria ever again in Venice. Just when there was a consciousness of the full range of traditions that could be drawn on in Venice, and an architect with the enthusiasm and the courage to try to pull them together into a new unity, there was a building in progress and at exactly the stage that allowed for subtle but fundamental

changes. These conditions occurred only once, and within a few years such a building had become impossible.

The churches considered so far indicate that through the 1480s church architecture in Venice was an amalgam of local and imported Gothic, Tuscan Romanesque, Albertian and, to some degree, Venetian Byzantine styles. What these buildings have in common is not so much their forms as their aspiration: the desire to draw a rich variety of traditions together in a new way. As a group of buildings they lack any internal coherence; each remains an isolated essay with only its synthetic intent in common with the others.

In the decade before 1500 there began to emerge a new trend in church architecture, clearer and more deeply rooted in a single Venetian tradition. For the first time we find a group of churches that has in common not only intent but also form, the result of a growing concentration on the Byzantine, represented primarily by San Marco (Figs. 8, 9), as the basis of a new Venetian style.

In the 15th century Italian architects began to seek

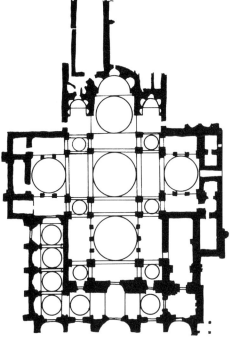

Fig. 8 San Marco. Nave, begun 1063

Fig. 9 San Marco. Plan (after W. L. MacDonald, *Early Christian and Byzantine Architecture*, 1965)

alternatives to the Gothic style, which they came to regard as something that had been imposed on them by foreigners. It is now generally agreed that Brunelleschi began the Florentine architectural Renaissance by using the Tuscan Romanesque to cleanse Florentine architecture of its Gothic elements. The Byzantine revival in Venice was a parallel attempt to forge a new style by skipping back over the Gothic interlude to a tradition with deep local roots.

The most important pre-Gothic building in Venice was San Marco. As the church of the Doge, its grip on the imagination of the Venetians and its place in their self-image were always very great; in the 15th century the church seems almost to have been identified with Venetian fortune.

To some extent the Byzantine revival owes its rise to the fall of Constantinople. There was a clear awareness among the Venetians of ties to Byzantium, and of being the heirs to her cultural and artistic traditions after 1453. The idea of a connection between Venice and Byzantium had a compelling architectural argument in San Marco, perhaps the most Byzantine church ever built in Italy.

If the fall of Constantinople had a sudden cultural impact, the major political problem of the late 15th century was the gradual alignment of much of Western Europe against the Venetian Republic, culminating in the formation of the League of Cambrai in the first decade of the 16th century. The self-image of Venice as the heir to Byzantium, combined with her estrangement from the Latin West, were given architectural expression in the Byzantine revival.

That San Marco was the source of this revival was recognized as early as the 1570s, when Francesco Sansovino described some of the churches as being based on the 'central cube' of San Marco. He meant the nine-cell, five-dome plan with a large dome in the central cell and four smaller ones in the corners of a circumscribed square (Figs. 9, 12). In the later 15th century the return to this clear and simple arrangement appears to have taken some time. We find with the churches of the Byzantine revival – begun mostly between 1494 and 1507 – a situation analogous to that which we observed in the gradual approximation of the design of the Arch of the Sergii in Venetian portals around 1460; it took a while before the San Marco plan was utilized in a clear and fairly straightforward manner.

The new interest in centralized domed spaces is not, however, the first example of the reconsideration of San Marco in the later 15th century. This church was a living source in Venice in the second half of the 15th century, and each generation, or even each decade, saw different possibilities in it. Before the 1490s architects were not yet ready to build according to a Byzantine central plan, but they looked carefully at other elements of San Marco.

The earliest work which reflects a reconsideration of San Marco is the chancel of San Giobbe (Plate 25), designed in the early 1470s. The pierced dome, among the earliest features of San Marco to be revived, was not to find a permanent place in the Byzantine revival; none of the centrally planned churches built later was lit in this manner.

At Santa Maria dei Miracoli (Plates 12, 28, 29), built in the 1480s, the rich marble revetment shows the influence of San Marco. This led to the idea that the Miracoli was built with marble left over from San Marco. There is no evidence for this – it seems to be a myth – but it is interesting how the story acknowledges and tries to account for the similarity.

In the upper parts of the nave and ambulatory of San Zaccaria, datable to the 1480s, we see a new interest in domed spaces. The sequence from the nave groin vaults to the nave dome to the half-dome of the choir to the ring of domes in the ambulatory is very impressive, despite its somewhat unintegrated character. This very un-Gothic shaping of space may have been inspired by the interior of San Marco.

Credit for the change from the adaptation of specific elements of San Marco to a thorough analysis of the style and possibilities of the building as a whole seems to go to Codussi. His is the dominant architectural intelligence in Venice in the last quarter of the 15th century and, after trying at San Michele and San Zaccaria to fuse a variety of traditions, he seems to have decided on another, more unified approach, experimenting with Byzantine centralized domed sequences.

The surviving churches that make up the Byzantine revival group are Santa Maria Formosa, begun by Codussi in 1492; San Giovanni Crisostomo, also by Codussi, begun in 1497; Santa Maria Mater Domini, apparently begun in 1504; San Salvatore, begun in 1506; San Fantino, apparently begun around 1507; San Giovanni Elemosinario, begun around 1525; and San Felice, begun around 1531.

Sansovino reports that in the 11th century Santa Maria Formosa (Fig. 10; Plates 9, 31) was rebuilt on the model of the 'central cube' of San Marco. It is difficult to see this in the

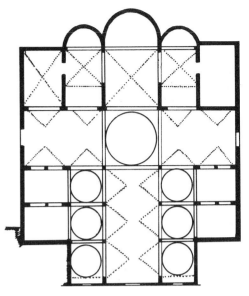

Fig. 10 Santa Maria Formosa, begun 1492. Mauro Codussi. Plan (after Paoletti)

Fig. 11 Florence: San Lorenzo. Nave, begun 1423. Filippo Brunelleschi. (*See Plate 9*)

19

present plan for, while the church is roughly centralized, the characteristic four small domes around the central cupola are absent. Instead we have a three-bay nave and two-bay transepts, with a dome at the crossing. Flanking the nave are aisles with domes on pendentives (Plate 31), and opening off the second and third bays of each aisle are barrel-vaulted chapels.

San Giovanni Crisostomo (Fig. 12; Plates 36–8) is much simpler and purer in plan than Santa Maria Formosa, with a clearer dependence on San Marco. The plan and vaulting system are much more consistent and centralized; here we find the basic nine-cell arrangement with a central cupola, four equal barrel-vaulted arms, and pendentive domes in the corners. To the east the choir and the two chapels that flank it extend from the nine-cell square.

At Santa Maria Mater Domini (Plates 39, 40) we have a major change. The thin and delicate quality of the Codussi buildings is gone. Piers now support arches while applied half-columns carry the entablature above. This Roman system had never been used for a Venetian nave elevation before, although it is found in the slightly earlier monks' gallery at San Michele in Isola (Plate 17). This change in style is interestingly analogous to the change from the style of Brunelleschi to that of Alberti in Florentine architecture of the third quarter of the 15th century.

As the nave elevation of Santa Maria Mater Domini makes a new departure, so does the façade (Plate 41), which may date from as late as the 1530s. Here the lobed silhouette was abandoned in favour of a triangular pediment and flanking concave volutes. The façade of San Sebastiano (Plate 35), which dates from the 1540s, was another attempt to find a different form for church façades.

The two churches of San Salvatore and San Fantino are closely related. San Salvatore (Fig. 13; Plate 42), begun in 1506, has an ingenious plan. In Spavento's design three San Marco 'cubes', overlapping at the corner domes, create a longitudinal church with a nave and aisles. Only slight extensions were required for the transepts, and apses at the ends of the nave and aisles complete the plan.

San Fantino (p. 6) has an uncertain building history. It seems a precursor to San Salvatore because its plan and vaulting system are less integrated, but it was begun a year later. The notion of lengthening a church by multiplying 'cubes' is considered, but not clearly developed; there is not a complete 'cube' anywhere in the plan. The groin vaults in the nave and small

aisle bays are old-fashioned; from the time of the design of San Giovanni Crisostomo ten years earlier, the preference had been for domes at these points. The choir of the church is later than the nave, and if the original design of San Fantino called for the choir to have a dome, perhaps the intention was to emphasize it by having groin vaults in the nave and aisles.

These five Byzantine revival churches all date from 1494 to 1507. After this period of activity there was a twenty-year hiatus in church building, due in part to Venetian wars with the League of Cambrai, and in part to the disastrous Rialto fire of 1514, which necessitated major reconstruction. San Giovanni Elemosinario (Plates 43, 44), destroyed in the fire, was not rebuilt until the mid-1520s, and dedicated in 1527. This church is in many respects quite boring and ineffectual: its plan is standard and gives no evidence of fresh thought, and the execution is clumsy. The Byzantine revival was waning.

The last of the Byzantine revival churches, and in some ways the most peculiar, is San Felice (Plates 45, 46). It was begun around 1531, but it is close in style to the Codussi churches of thirty-five years earlier, having little in common with those begun after 1500.

By the 1530s the Byzantine revival was finished. Sansovino's churches of the mid-16th century, large undivided squares covered with flat ceilings (Fig. 14), are very different from the domed nine-cell central plans inspired by San Marco. They are not without Venetian precedents, however, for the single-nave church with a high-altar chapel and two lower flanking chapels is known from San Giobbe, San Rocco and San Sebastiano. It is characteristic of Venetian church architecture that the type which replaced the Byzantine revival church, although developed by a non-Venetian, was rooted in the local tradition.

Chapels

Virtually all the private chapels built in Venice in the period under consideration here were attached to churches and opened off the interior of the main building. Usually these chapels were later additions to their host churches; only rarely was a transept converted to a family chapel (Plate 50). Venetian chapels tended to be rectangular in plan, and rather open extensions of the space of the church; the decoration of these projecting structures was almost always restricted to their interiors (Plates

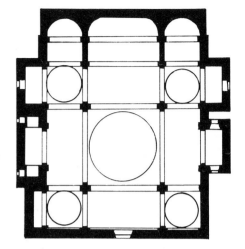

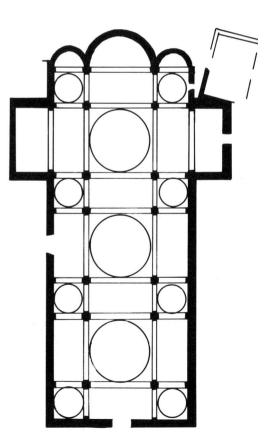

The Cornaro Chapel in Santi Apostoli (Plate 49) is quite different in character. The carving is much more severe than that of the Gussoni Chapel, and the emphasis is on the relationship between the walls, corner columns, entablature, pendentive arches and dome as coherent parts of a system which is conceived architecturally rather than as a vehicle for sculptural elaboration.

The Bernabò Chapel in San Giovanni Crisostomo (Plate 50) is an interesting combination of architecture and narrative sculpture, and the similarity between the space represented in Tullio Lombardo's relief of *The Coronation of the Virgin* on the altar and the actual space of the chapel is unique in Venice in this period.

The Emiliana Chapel at San Michele in Isola (Plates 51, 52) which dates from about twenty-five years after the completion of the Bernabò Chapel, is the only chapel of this period with a fully articulated exterior. It is physically more distinct from its church than any of the others are, and is not entered directly from the church, but through a small pentagonal vestibule. Although a chapel, in many ways it can be regarded as a different sort of building from the wide, rectangular chapels that open off church naves.

Palace Façades

The word *palazzo* is not one which figured much in Venetian descriptions of houses in the 15th and 16th centuries. The Palazzo Ducale was called the *palazzo*, but Venetian houses, even the large and important ones, were usually called *cà*, a dialect shortening of *casa* (house). Just as there was only one *piazza* in Venice, that of San Marco, and all the other urban spaces were *campi*, there was only one palace, and all other domestic buildings were houses. In many cases, despite the 19th-century tendency to call every large or elegant house a palace, the earlier Venetian usage survives, and is still applied to some very big and lavish buildings, such as the Cà d'Oro, Cà del Duca and Cà Foscari, or the huge 17th-century Cà Pesaro and Cà Rezzonico.

The most distinctive feature of Venetian palaces is the total absence of fortifications. In this the owners of private palaces took their cue from the Palazzo Ducale (Plate 93) which, with its lacy walls and vulnerable arcades, is totally unlike mainland

Far left
Fig. 12 San Giovanni Crisostomo, begun 1497. Mauro Codussi. Plan (after Paoletti)

Fig. 13 San Salvatore, begun 1506. Giorgio Spavento. Plan (after Paoletti)

Left
Fig. 14 San Giuliano, begun 1566. Interior. Jacopo Sansovino

47–9). Nonetheless, the chapels were usually treated as independent architectural entities, and generally there was no attempt to make their decoration consistent with that of the church to which they were connected. This was the case even when the transept of a small church was treated as a chapel. Only one important chapel was given any sort of elaborate exterior treatment (Plate 51), and in this case, while the interior was totally different in style from the contiguous church, the exterior was, in some important respects, made to correspond with the church façade.

The earliest chapel illustrated here, the Martini Chapel in San Giobbe (Plate 47), is exceptional among 15th-century Venetian chapels in its very strong Florentine flavour, but it had little or no effect on contemporary chapel design.

Three later chapels, all dating from around 1500, are much more Venetian in style, but they nonetheless vary widely.

The Gussoni Chapel in San Lio (Plate 48) is extensively carved – the pilasters, cornices, friezes and arches are all covered with lavish carvings in the style of Pietro Lombardo. The interest in rich textures extends to the vault, where we find a ribbed melon dome, rare in Venice. Like the same family's nearby palace (Plate 61), also attributed to Pietro Lombardo, the Gussoni Chapel is small, but makes up in elegant and extensive detail what it lacks in size.

Italian city halls. This was certainly an expression of confidence in the ability of the Venetian navy to protect the lagoon, in the stability of civic institutions and in the orderliness of the Venetian citizenry. The elegant and defenceless Venetian palaces were a matter of pride to the city; while fortresses tend to look alike, Venetian palaces do not, and in the 15th century façades in the city were more interesting and varied than in any other place in Italy.

In the 19th century, palaces were studied almost exclusively from the outside. It was characteristic of that century, concerned above all with appearances, to be interested mostly in exteriors, but this is not simply a quaint habit of mind. Frequently a façade establishes its own scale and character which have little to do with the style and distribution of rooms behind it. Façades were often regular and symmetrical when interiors were not.

The Venetian palace façade is a frontispiece applied to the principal exterior wall; its design was almost never carried to the sides of the building. The Palazzo Corner-Spinelli (Plate 63) is typical in this regard: its flanks are plain walls with simple windows. In Venice the attention, costly materials, architectural thought and social competition were directed almost exclusively to the façades. The decoration of palace courtyards in the 15th century centred on the external staircase from the ground floor to the *piano nobile*, but although there are some interesting and unusual treatments of staircases, such as that of the Palazzo Minelli (Plate 55), the façades are the most important parts of palaces.

The ground-plan of Venetian palaces, particularly those along the Grand Canal, was a function of real estate values in the city. Footage was more expensive there than on the streets or smaller canals, and palaces on the Grand Canal tended to be relatively narrow and deep. While there are some shallow palaces with very wide façades, such as the Palazzo Zorzi (Plate 59), they are not usually found on the Grand Canal.

Although there is less stylistic variety to be found in palaces than in churches, palace architecture is not uncomplicated. Alongside very progressive designs, strong reactionary tendencies are sometimes observed. The primary stylistic ingredients are Gothic and Classical; in contrast to church architecture, there is little evidence of a Byzantine revival in palaces.

It is clear from the Cà d'Oro (Fig. 15), begun in the

Fig. 15 Cà d'Oro. Façade, begun 1421

1420s, and the Palazzo Vendramin-Calergi (Plate 64), finished around 1508, that in the eighty-five years or so that separate the two façades some major stylistic changes took place. Strong asymmetry, richly decorated surfaces and contrasting treatments of each storey gave way to perfect symmetry, Classical vocabulary and more uniform treatment. While it is true to say that the façades show a change from florid late Gothic to a Classical revival, from a style dominated by variety to one dominated by regularity, this explains little about the process by which style was transformed.

The changes between these two façades fall into four categories: from asymmetry to symmetry; from loose to very exact vertical alignment of the façade elements; from varied to uniform treatment of the decoration in all levels of the building; and from Gothic to Classical decorative elements. The development of palace façades in the 15th century sometimes seems irregular because these changes are hardly ever parallel. Some palaces have exactly symmetrical façades with no vertical alignment of elements through all the storeys, such as the Palazzo Corner

Spinelli (Plate 63) and the Palazzo Manzoni-Angaran (Plate 65). There are façades in which some storeys are symmetrically arranged and others not – there can be either a symmetrical ground level under asymmetrical upper storeys, as at the Cà Dario (Plate 16), or symmetrical upper levels over a ground storey with an eccentric entrance. We find buildings with rather Classical decoration which are very asymmetrical, such as the Cà Dario, and perfectly symmetrical façades with Gothic decoration, such as the Palazzo dell'Ambasciatore (Plate 13), as well as odd combinations of both Gothic and Classical, such as the Palazzo Morolin (Plate 58). Sometimes exteriors are of brick with stone decoration (Plate 53), sometimes entirely of Istrian stone and marble, such as the Palazzo Contarini delle Figure (Plate 68), and sometimes revetted and inlaid with strongly veined polychrome marble and other rich stones, such as the Cà Dario (Plate 16). The possibilities are nearly limitless.

While most of the palaces considered here are large, there are many interesting domestic buildings in Venice on a modest scale. Sometimes the owner of a small, ordinary and not well-situated house could afford to have it embellished in the latest style to make it more impressive than its neighbours. The Palazzo Gussoni (Plate 61) is an example of this sort. No bigger than many completely unadorned buildings (Plate 62), it distinguishes itself by its decoration, and is as indicative of the attitudes and aspirations of its owner as the largest and most imposing palaces of the time.

One of the most interesting and still only partly understood Venetian palaces is the huge, unfinished Cà del Duca (Plate 57), which dates from the beginning of our period. The architect, Bartolomeo Buon, had worked at the Cà d'Oro with his father Giovanni, but at the Cà del Duca he turned dramatically from the floriated Gothic. The small portion of the building that was built shows a number of non-Venetian elements. The Cà del Duca seems to have had too many new and foreign ideas in it to influence Venetian palace architecture of the third quarter of the 15th century, which was on the whole rather traditional; we do not find in palaces of this period the same active experimentation with many forms that we find in church design.

The loggia of the Palazzo Ducale was probably completed by 1360, but its particular tracery system was not widely copied in Venetian palaces until about 1450. The *piano nobile* of the Cà d'Oro (Fig. 15) is an elaboration of the Palazzo Ducale loggia but, in an interesting reversal of what we might expect,

the Palazzo Ducale scheme is more exactly repeated only in the next generation. Around 1440 it began to appear in the main windows of many palaces, such as the Palazzo Bernardo (Plate 53) and the Palazzo dell'Ambasciatore (Plate 13). At the same time that a century-old pattern was being repeated, a new one was emerging. Implied in the upper storey of the Cà d'Oro, this new type, which appeared around 1450, is seen in the upper storey of the Palazzo Pisani-Moretta (Plate 54). Thus, in the same years that the Cà del Duca offered an alternative to local traditions, Venetian architects were still elaborating late Gothic tracery for palace façades. This range of stylistic possibilities is similar to, if less broad, than what we have observed in churches of the third quarter of the century.

The storeys of Venetian palaces were treated in a number of ways. Usually the *piano nobile* has the richest tracery, and the storey above only simple trefoiled windows, as at the Palazzo dell'Ambasciatore, but sometimes a higher floor was more elaborate, as at the Palazzo Bernardo. Very rich façades had full tracery on the two upper levels, as at the Cà d'Oro and the Palazzo Pisano-Moretta, where the patterns are different on each level.

It is against the background of the palaces of 1450 to 1480 that we must see the Palazzo Corner-Spinelli (Plate 63). Datable to the 1480s and attributed to Codussi, the palace was executed in a new vocabulary and according to a new system. In none of the earlier façades do we find identical window treatment on two levels, as we do here. At the Palazzo Corner-Spinelli orders are applied to the façade in an unprecedented way for Venice. As early as the mid-14th century the upper-storey corners of the Palazzo Ducale had been decorated with tall and slender twisted colonnettes. This was continued at the Cà d'Oro as well as in many other buildings of the later 15th century, such as the Palazzo dell'Ambasciatore, where the colonnettes rise from the foundations to the upper cornices, but even if they sometimes have a base and a capital at each storey, there is very very little of the Classical about them. At the Palazzo Corner-Spinelli, on the other hand, there are full Classical pilasters at the edges of the façade.

At the Palazzo Vendramin-Calergi (Plate 64), also attributed to Codussi and begun *c.* 1500, the system is much more sophisticated than at the Palazzo Corner-Spinelli, for there are pilasters on the ground storey and columns in the two above. Double orders mark the edges of the façade and separate the central section from the flanking ones; single orders separate the windows of the central section from each other. Despite its Classical vocabulary, this arrangement still retains something of the distribution of elements seen earlier in the façade of the Palazzo dell'Ambasciatore, for example, with a wide central section and two flanking ones. This is quite different from the very regular distribution of windows in Florentine palaces of even sixty years earlier.

The Palazzo Corner-Spinelli and the Palazzo Vendramin-Calergi indicate one line of façade development, but there is another, represented here by three works. The earliest, the Palazzo Manzoni-Angaran (Plate 65), begun *c.* 1485, has single pilasters at the edges of the façade and flanking the central section; each storey is divided into three sections. There are no pilasters between the windows of the central section and there is no tracery in them.

At the Palazzo Contarini delle Figure (Plate 68) we find pilasters flanking the central section of the façade, and here the three sections are much more even in size than at the Palazzo Manzoni-Angaran. The decoration is also very different from the Palazzo Manzoni-Angaran, with more complex window frames and a series of triangular pediments placed across the *piano nobile.*

At the Palazzo Grimani a San Polo (Plate 69) the façade is divided rather evenly into three sections and the entablature of each storey breaks over the pilasters below it, giving all the important horizontal elements a similar treatment. This was never popular in Venice, but it indicates a concern to organize the façade in a completely consistent manner.

From the Palazzo Corner-Spinelli to the Palazzo Vendramin-Calergi there is a development toward a style of fully sculpted, densely packed elements tightly framed in a strong system of emphatic horizontals and verticals. The Palazzo Manzoni-Angaran, the Palazzo Contarini delle Figure and the Palazzo Grimani a San Polo, on the other hand, reveal an interest in more open and even divisions of the façade in which the relief, although at times strong, is always read against the flat and neutral plane of the wall.

The stylistic range of palace façades of the first third of the 16th century indicates that the Venetian interest in a wide variety of arrangements within a general type, observed in the Gothic palaces of the mid-15th century, was still a major force. By 1500 Gothic vocabulary was no longer a stylistic element in palace façades but, despite the change from Gothic to Classical, the Venetian fondness for varied effects and contrasts both subtle and strong is maintained. Venetians never desired consistency, let alone uniformity, among their buildings.

Scuole

The *scuole* were very important social institutions in Venice. They were not schools in the usual sense, but confraternities whose primary function was service to the poor. The earliest of the six so-called *scuole grandi*, including the Scuola San Marco and the Scuola San Giovanni Evangelista, were founded in the mid-13th century; the latest, San Rocco, in 1480. In time, several of these became very wealthy organizations, and undertook construction of large and sometimes sumptuous quarters.

To understand the architecture of the *scuole* it is crucial to recognize the extremely strong and often frankly expressed sense of competition among them. If one *scuola* made an architectural advance it was quite common for the others to copy it quickly and unambiguously; after a double-ramp staircase had been built at the Scuola San Marco the brethren of the Scuola San Giovanni Evangelista hired the man who executed it to do one like it for them. If this is the most blatant example of imitation it is not the only one, and because of this competition, by the middle of the 16th century *scuole* buildings had come to resemble each other in several important ways.

The earliest major example of *scuola* architecture in our period was the atrium at the Scuola San Giovanni Evangelista (Plate 81), which is dated 1481 and attributed to Pietro Lombardo. This *scuola* was situated in rather cramped quarters, only gradually acquiring small pieces of land for its expansion, and could never engage in a large-scale building programme. In the 15th and early 16th centuries its additions tended therefore to be small and elegant.

The largest building campaign among the *scuole* in the late 15th century was at the Scuola San Marco. In 1485 the *scuola* was heavily damaged by fire, and in its reconstructed form included several important innovations. The façade (Plate 66) was lavishly decorated, perhaps in competitive response to the atrium of the Scuola San Giovanni Evangelista finished only a few years before; it is interesting that Pietro Lombardo, who – as mentioned above – appears to have done the Scuola San

Fig. 16 Palazzo Grimani a San Luca, begun *c.* 1556. Michele Sanmichele. (*See Plate 64*)

Giovanni atrium, was later hired at the Scuola San Marco to carry out the façade decoration there.

The Scuola San Marco is divided into two parts which had different functions: the left side contained the large *piano nobile* meeting hall (Plate 72), while the right, known as the *albergo*, housed a smaller council chamber. The ground-floor hall of the left side was given an innovative double colonnade (Plate 72) running from the main façade on the *campo* back to a water entrance on a small canal. Access to the upper floor is by way of a double-ramp staircase. Formed like an inverted V, two ramps rise from each end of the long lower hall, providing easy approaches from both the street and water entrances (Plate 76), to meet on a landing aligned with the centre of the upper hall (Plate 77).

The problems of style and documentation of the façade are complex, and deserve a close look. Pietro Lombardo and Buora went to work as *proti* of the *scuola* some time in 1488 or 1489, after reconstruction had begun. In late 1490 Codussi replaced them. At the time the brick walls of the building were largely complete, as was the decoration of the lower zone of the exterior. A major question is whether the stylistic differences between the ground floor and upper levels are part of a single design, or are to be explained by the change of architect.

There are, to be sure, sharp changes in the decorative style of the second storey, but the fluted pilasters, vases with flames, and even the round tympanum over the main portal are all known from Pietro's atrium of the Scuola San Giovanni Evangelista. The decoration of the crowning tympana, particularly the three on the left side, resembles other work by Codussi – the entablature and the arch of the central tympanum are close in detail to the upper parts of the façades of San Zaccaria and the Palazzo Vendramin-Calergi (Plates 8, 64) and were certainly carried out by him. The trilobed silhouette of the left side, which in some respects resembles Codussi's church façades, has suggested to some that he designed the uppermost sections of the entire façade. But we know that Buora used the system found on the right side of the façade in another work (Plate 78). Evidence that Codussi did not dramatically alter the façade is found in the way the ground level of the left half, with the tympanum over the main portal extending into the storey above, is perfectly echoed in the silhouette of its uppermost level. The ground-floor sequence surely dates from before Codussi's arrival on the job, and so likely does its echo.

It is sometimes suggested that the *piano nobile* windows are by Codussi; they are more complex in form than anything we know by Pietro Lombardo before this time, especially those on the left side of the façade. While this attribution is not certain, we do know that Codussi made some changes at this level. A large relief for the centre *piano nobile* bay of the left side, mentioned in the last contract with Pietro and Buora, was never put in place, but whether its elimination was due to the new architect or a shortage of money is unclear.

Some details of the façade decoration must be attributed to Codussi, such as the columns in the uppermost sections of the left side and the lion heads in the pilasters of this level, both of which recall the façade of San Zaccaria (Plate 8). When all of this evidence is considered it seems most likely that in its general form the entire façade had been determined before Codussi took over the project, but that he modified many of the details.

The most influential part of the Scuola San Marco reconstruction was its double-ramp staircase, also planned well before Codussi arrived to execute it. It has been dramatically altered; only the entrance portals (Plates 76, 77) are fully preserved.

There is little question that in 1498 Codussi was commissioned to construct a similar but grander double-ramp staircase at the Scuola San Giovanni Evangelista because of rivalry with the Scuola San Marco. He did not disappoint his patrons; he produced one of the most beautiful staircases to be seen anywhere, and one of the glories of Venetian architecture (Plates 67, 83-5).

The new staircase was built next to the earlier *scuola* buildings on a narrow strip of land that the confraternity had just succeeded in acquiring from neighbours. A water entrance was built at the bottom of one ramp so that the staircase had the same function it did at the Scuola San Marco. The space available for the new work was slightly irregular, narrower at the ends than at the centre. This happy accident allowed Codussi to make the staircase wider at the top. From below, a tall and narrow staircase of uniform width would appear by natural perspective effect to grow smaller as it rose. Able to widen the staircase increasingly toward the top, Codussi counteracted this effect, giving the ramps the appearance of greater size than would otherwise have been the case.

In his second staircase Codussi followed his own particular line of inquiry into the combination of vaulted and domed spaces. He eliminated the domes over the mid-flight landings that had appeared in the Scuola San Marco staircase, giving a clear indication of his genius – rather than elaborating shapes or pointlessly multiplying domes, he simplified the sequence when doing so would clarify the ideas of a design and convey them more effectively. In a certain sense we might understand the San Giovanni staircase as an extension, into a work on more than one storey, of the ideas that Codussi first began to develop at Santa Maria Formosa (Plates 9, 31). There, small domes on pendentives in the aisles function almost as sockets around which a shift of axis takes place from the longitudinal and vertical nave to the transverse and horizontal chapels. At the Scuola San Giovanni we find a similar sequence in the staircase, but in a much more coherent system. The vaulting system of the Scuola San Giovanni staircase can be understood as the expression of the only possible direction taken by a visitor in the ascent to the upper floor of the building.

The ground-floor portal of the Scuola San Giovanni (Plate 82) dates from after Codussi's death, and represents the style of a later generation of architects.

The Scuola San Rocco was begun in 1517 by Bono and had three other architects before it was finished in the late 1540s. In many ways it is based on the Scuola San Marco; we find the same two-part façade (Plate 86), the same double-colonnaded ground-floor hall with the columns set on high pedestals (Plate 87), land and water entrances at opposite ends of the main ground-floor hall, and a double-ramp staircase (Plates 88, 89), although of a slightly different type from those built by Codussi.

In both buildings we find columns flanking the main doorway and lining up with the ground-floor colonnades. Perhaps the *piano nobile* window columns at San Rocco, with their tall cylindrical bases, derive ultimately from the portal columns of the Scuola San Marco (Plate 66). The ground-floor windows at the Scuola San Rocco, on the other hand, derive from the staircase landing window at the Scuola San Giovanni Evangelista (Plate 85). In its vocabulary the Scuola San Rocco is very different from the Scuola San Marco, and its strong façade relief, for example, shows a 16th-century style which is totally at odds with the earlier work. In its general organization and in some of its details, however, the building is based on a clear *scuola* type that was established in the last two decades of the 15th century.

Civic Buildings

While Venetian civic buildings of our period shared the same patron, they vary in style and meaning from the Scala dei Giganti in the Palazzo Ducale (Plate 79) to the Clock Tower in Piazza San Marco (Plate 74), from the Arsenale portal (Plate 70) to the Rialto Fabbriche Vecchie (Plate 102). In considering them, a number of functions, forms and traditions must be taken into account, as well as Venetian political iconography and the constantly shifting financial circumstances of the period. When conditions permitted, Venetian civic architecture could be lavish; on occasion, when money was tight, buildings were severe, almost purely utilitarian. Questions of propaganda sometimes enter the picture. In a time of financial and political difficulty the Venetians built the Clock Tower to impress friend and foe alike with their resources.

The period between 1450 and 1540 saw the fullest flowering of civic building in the history of Venice. The major work was done in two parts of the city. The most important by far was the area around San Marco, where the work was carried out in the Palazzo Ducale as well as in the buildings around the Piazza (Fig. 17). By the end of the period the San Marco area had been transformed entirely, and taken on almost all of its

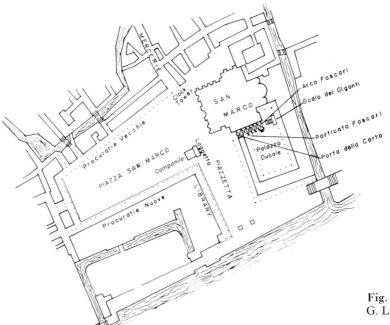

Fig. 17 Piazza San Marco. Plan (after G. Lorenzetti, *Venice and Its Lagoon*, 1961)

present appearance. The secondary centre of activity was at Rialto, where a fire of 1505 necessitated the construction of a new Fondaco dei Tedeschi, and a much worse one in 1514 required the almost total rebuilding of the city's primary banking and market centre.

The Palazzo Ducale was built in several stages and has a rather complex history. The south wing was begun in 1340; the west wing, continuing the design of the south, was begun in the 1420s. In the late 1430s the contract for the Porta della Carta (Fig. 18) was signed, as well as for the Porticato Foscari, the tunnel that leads back towards the east wing of the palace (Figs. 17, 18). The east end of this tunnel was given considerable elaboration in the Arco Foscari (Plate 71).

The east wing of the Palazzo Ducale was severely damaged by fire in 1483, and in the reconstruction between the mid-1480s and the early 16th century that part of the palace was entirely rebuilt in a richly decorative style. To this period belong the Scala dei Giganti (Plate 79) and the design of both the courtyard and canal façades of the east wing (Plates 90, 91). Slightly later, around 1520, the north façade of the courtyard on the Cortiletto dei Senatori was built (Plate 92).

Around the Piazza San Marco building activity began haltingly with repair work to the Campanile (Plate 75) after it was struck by lightning in 1489, but got underway seriously with the construction of the Clock Tower (Plate 74), built between 1496 and 1499 and then widened by the addition of lateral wings in the first years of the 16th century. A few years later the building next to it along the north side of the Piazza, the Procuratie Vecchie, built in the late 12th century (Plates 94, 95), was torn down and replaced (Plates 96, 97). The Piazzetta was regularized slightly later, beginning in the 1530s, with the construction of the Library designed by Sansovino (Plate 99), and the east side of the base of the Campanile was embellished by the addition of Sansovino's Loggetta (Plate 98). Late in the 16th century the wall system of the Library was continued down the south side of the Piazza as the façade of the Procuratie Nuove.

The Piazza and the Piazzetta form one of the most famous urban spaces in the world. There is no question that the organized variety of the area as it was at the end of the 16th century, although it had taken by then over four hundred years to achieve, had been thought out very carefully. Its basic organizing principle is the establishment of clearly defined and framed

Fig. 18 Palazzo Ducale. Porta della Carta, looking towards the Scala dei Giganti. Begun 1438. Bartolomeo Buon

axes accented at each end and flanked by buildings which are balanced and related to each other but different in style. It is difficult to establish exactly when this idea began to evolve. There are signs that it had been a factor as early as the 12th century, but it fully emerged as the guiding idea in the last years of the 15th century and the first third of the 16th. Once this principle is recognized, the almost miraculous cohesiveness of the area, despite the centuries it took to build and the widely varying styles of the buildings that make it up, becomes comprehensible.

The two principal axes, almost exactly equal in length, run roughly east-west along the Piazza and north-south along the Piazzetta (Fig. 17; Plate 95). Opposite the church of San Marco, at the west end of the Piazza, was, until the early 19th century, the small church of San Geminiano, which had been built in the 13th century but rebuilt on a central plan beginning in 1505. This church was the only central-plan church of the period to be given lavish interior decoration with extensive marble revetment, and it formed an appropriate focus at the other end of the Piazza from San Marco. It did not matter that the two churches, while related in plan, were not at all similar in size or in the style of their exteriors; their differences seem in fact to have been regarded very positively, for they created a lively variety.

The Clock Tower (Plate 74) established a focus at the north end of the Piazzetta opposite the two columns that had stood at the south end since the 12th century (Plates 93, 95). Until it was built in the 1490s there had been no strong focus of the view up the Piazzetta; there were only the arches of the 12th-century Procuratie Vecchie (Plate 94). The Clock Tower was originally only one bay wide, but soon after it was built it was widened by two bays on each side. Perhaps the original design, while it functioned perfectly as a support for the clock and the bell above, was too small to focus the view up the Piazzetta, and was widened out of purely visual considerations.

Within the axial organization of the large-scale elements in the San Marco area are some very subtle arrangements on a smaller scale which are both visually stunning and highly symbolic for Venice. One of the most remarkable architectural sequences anywhere in Italy is to be found on the axis that leads from the Campanile and Loggetta through the Porta della Carta, down the Porticato Foscari, out through the Arco Foscari and up the Scala dei Giganti (Fig. 17). This axis first began to take shape with the construction of the west wing of the Palazzo Ducale in the 1420s. In the 1440s the Porta della Carta and the Porticato Foscari were under construction, and around 1450 the eastern end of the tunnel was embellished by the first phase of the Arco Foscari (Plate 71). With the reconstruction of the east wing of the palace after the fire of 1483, the Scala dei Giganti (Plate 79) provided the eastern focus of the axis with a monumental stone staircase.

In the early years of the 16th century the south flank of San Marco, which forms the north end of the Piazzetta (visible in Plate 75), was altered in a way that strongly suggests it was regarded increasingly as the back-drop to the Scala dei Giganti-Campanile axis that runs across the area right in front of it. Until 1504 the main ceremonial entrance to the Basilica was through the south end of the narthex. This entry was closed when the Chapel of Cardinal Zen was built in the southern-most bay of the narthex (Fig. 9). The exterior of the filled-in arch was given rich marble treatment to make it effective as a wall against which processions would be seen. The closing of the old entrance to the church with the Zen Chapel in 1504 eliminated what must have come to be regarded as a major distraction on the strong ceremonial way.

Sansovino's Loggetta (Plate 98) on the east side of the Campanile completed the sequence by providing the western focus. The entire axis is brilliantly clear and effective. The Scala dei Giganti and the Loggetta face each other through the Porticato Foscari. Facing each of these is a monumental gateway. The Porta della Carta faces the Loggetta and the Arco Foscari faces the Scala dei Giganti so that there are two shorter axes within the longer one. The main axis becomes more impressive and intelligent when we consider the itinerary of official visitors to Venice. One of the primary sights of the city was the view from the top of the Campanile; it is said that important guests of the Republic were permitted to ride up the spiral interior ramp of the Campanile on mule back. At each end of the great Venetian ceremonial axis there were therefore major ascents; to the east up the Scala dei Giganti to the ducal apartments, state reception rooms, and the centre of power of the Republic; to the west, to the top of the Campanile to look out over all of Venice and to the two areas of her dominion, the sea and the *terra firma*. Whether such a programme was planned as early as the 1440s is difficult to determine. The Campanile was already standing by then, and perhaps the placement of the Porta della Carta and the Porticato Foscari was made with this axis in mind. With the construction of each new element the sequence grew clearer and more compelling. Once the Scala dei Giganti had established the eastern end, it remained only to elaborate the base of the Campanile. It is beyond question that by the time Sansovino was at work on the Loggetta the entire axis had come to be regarded as part of a coherent design, for it was he who added to the Scala dei Giganti the colossal figures of Mars and Neptune (Plate 79), balancing the antique programme of the Loggetta with more explicit Classical symbols of Venetian land and sea power than had appeared there before.

The Loggetta is in part a ceremonial entrance to the Campanile, as the Scala dei Giganti is to the palace. Sansovino, who was familiar with Roman architecture, did not need Venetian examples to suggest to him that an entrance of some importance could be treated as a triumphal arch, but it is worth noting that the triumphal-arch motif of the Loggetta perfectly balances the triumphal-arch idea already expressed in the three round arches at the top of the Scala dei Giganti. The Loggetta completes with remarkable logic a double-ended *via triumphalis* rich in symbolic significance for the Republic.

At Rialto the important building activity in our period began with the reconstruction of the Fondaco dei Tedeschi (Plates 100, 101). This combination bank, office building, warehouse and hotel for German merchants and visitors in Venice was destroyed by fire in 1505. The speed with which it was rebuilt (the roof was already under way in 1506) is a measure of how much Venetians wanted to keep the Germans happy and friendly. At exactly this time the Pope and the kings of France and Spain had begun to ally against Venice, and the Venetians tried desperately to woo the Germans away from joining that alliance. Their hopes were dashed when Emperor Maximilian I formed an alliance with the Pope in 1507, and eventually joined the European-wide League of Cambrai against Venice.

The Fondaco was designed by one Jerome of Augsburg, who was chosen by the German merchants, but it was executed by Scarpagnino. The outside was elaborately decorated with frescoes by Giorgione and Titian which have long since faded away. The idea of a 'painted house' is German, not Venetian, and reflects the preferences and traditions of the people for whom the city built it. While this suggests that the Venetian government could take a very flexible approach to buildings for political motives, it must not be forgotten that the decision to fresco the exterior of the Fondaco dei Tedeschi was also a shrewd economizing measure. Giorgione received 150 ducats for his frescoes, far less than any sort of elaborate carving or marble or stone revetment would have cost.

In 1514 a terrible fire devastated most of the Rialto area on the side of the Grand Canal opposite the Fondaco dei Tedeschi. Although some very grand designs were submitted for its reconstruction, hard times required that the architecture of the market loggias and city offices (Plate 103) be kept simple and inexpensive. A few years later conditions had improved sufficiently for the Palazzo dei Camerlenghi (Plate 102), completed in the mid-1520s, to be given a rather richly carved exterior. It was the last important Venetian building to be decorated in the Lombard style. The Palazzo dei Camerlenghi, directly across the Grand Canal from the Fondaco dei Tedeschi, may to some extent have been designed as a pendant to the richly painted façade of the Fondaco; the fondness for balanced contrasts of material and decoration across open space, which we saw in the Piazza San Marco, would have been observed here as well.

The Architects

In view of the problems of chronology and attribution which plague the study of Venetian architecture it is not surprising that the artistic personalities of individual architects are often unclear. Of the architects who worked in Venice between 1450 and the arrival of Jacopo Sansovino in 1527, not one is as clearly known and understood as we would like. Nevertheless, we can form a full enough picture of individuals to recognize that while there were several competent men and one or two very skilled designers, only one, Mauro Codussi, was an architect of genius. The buildings of his closest contemporaries, Antonio Rizzo and Pietro Lombardo, are often attractive and elegant, but they depend for effect primarily on the richness of their materials and carving. The difference between the east courtyard façade of the Palazzo Ducale (Plate 90), on which both Rizzo and Pietro worked, and Codussi's Palazzo Vendramin-Calergi (Plate 64), is the difference between a rich brocade of Classical decorative elements and a clear and coherent architectural system.

Pietro added the raised choir to the barrel-vaulted nave of Santa Maria dei Miracoli (Plate 29), and while its extensive carving is sumptuous and satisfying, the interior spaces are awkward and disorienting. Codussi's architectural spaces, in contrast, are among the most stunning in Venice. His ability to organize internal sequences of focused variety was unrivalled in his time, and seldom matched later.

A somewhat elusive figure working in Venice from the mid-1480s until his death in 1509 was Giorgio Spavento, whose design for San Salvatore (Fig. 13; Plate 42) is extremely attractive and intelligent. For the last five years of his life Spavento worked closely with Antonio Scarpagnino; in 1505 Spavento had been given the position of *proto* of the Fondaco dei Tedeschi, but he handed it over to Scarpagnino, who made his first appearance on that project. Because Spavento saw to it that Scarpagnino was paid twice the usual amount for this work, it is safe to assume that Scarpagnino was Spavento's protégé, and had perhaps even come to Venice from Lombardy at Spavento's invitation. Scarpagnino had a long career in Venice, and built a number of things in the city. At his best he was dependable and competent, but only very seldom original. Some buildings, such as San Giovanni Elemosinario (Plates 43, 44), are really quite weak and unappealing while others, such as the façade of San Sebastiano (Plate 35), are interesting if also a bit awkward and unintegrated. The best work connected with Scarpagnino is the north façade of the Palazzo Ducale courtyard (Plate 91), where Spavento is documented as working in the first decade of the 16th century. The style of the *piano nobile* suggests a date in the 1520s, so the work is therefore to be given to Scarpagnino, but it is not impossible that it incorporates some of Spavento's ideas. This was one of a few projects on which both men worked.

Bartolomeo Bono spent much of his career executing the designs of others, as at the Campanile of San Marco (Plate 75) and the Procuratie Vecchie (Plates 96, 97). His church of San Rocco (Plates 32, 33) was radically altered in the 18th century, and only one part now remains. Bono's major work, the Scuola San Rocco (Plates 86–9), has a complex building history and it is not always possible to isolate Bono's ideas from those of the men who followed him. What can be established is that, in the Scuola San Rocco at least, he followed and, in a heavier 16th-century style, developed Codussi's ideas for the Scuola San Marco and the Scuola San Giovanni Evangelista, but this dependence may have been a result of that particular commission rather than reflecting his general style.

In terms of a cluster of architectural works of very great quality, the period between the construction of the Palazzo Vendramin-Calergi and the Library of San Marco is, with few exceptions, something of an anticlimax. However, this is only because the astonishing quality of the Codussi buildings sets a standard that is very difficult to match. One of the great wonders of Venetian architecture is Codussi's series of late works. In the six years before his death in 1504, he crowned his achievements in church, staircase and palace design, and created three of the city's greatest buildings. At San Giovanni Crisostomo, he clarified and rationalized the ideas he had first explored at Santa Maria Formosa. In the staircase of the Scuola San Giovanni Evangelista he further developed and extended ideas from the Scuola San Marco. In the façade of the Palazzo Vendramin-Calergi he carried the ideas of the Palazzo Corner-Spinelli forward into a much more subtle and intelligent style. In the last years of his life Codussi had reached a level so far beyond his contemporaries that he could learn only from himself. The accomplishment of his late works constitutes one of the strongest and most varied contributions to Venetian architecture made by anyone up to that time. Perhaps only Sansovino later in the 16th century or Longhena in the 17th could be regarded as his equals in this respect.

The High Renaissance

While most of the architects who worked in Venice from 1450 to 1530 were foreigners, they were all from either Lombardy or the Veneto, where a strongly Classical style never dominated the local architecture. When Bartolomeo Bono died in 1529, he was replaced as *proto* of the Procurators of San Marco, the most important single architectural post in the city, not by another Lombard or a Venetian, but by the Florentine Sansovino, who had worked in Rome until the sack of 1527. With the exodus of artists from the Papal capital that year the High Renaissance style, largely a Roman amalgam, was diffused throughout Italy. If the Early Renaissance in Venice was an experimental attitude toward architectural traditions and possibilities, the High Renaissance was more a style in the traditional sense, characterized by greater certainty, hence much less pronounced variety, and dominated by a consistent classicism.

At the time of Sansovino's arrival in Venice the city had been drained financially by the wars with the League of Cambrai and the massive reconstruction required after the terrible Rialto fire of 1514. The Venetian architectural imagination too seems to have been exhausted; the Palazzo dei Camerlenghi and the church of San Giovanni Elemosinario, both of which date from the mid-1520s, indicate that old forms were being repeated rather mechanically. With the appointment of Sansovino Venetian architecture began a steady turn toward a more severely Classical Roman manner. While this direction had been anticipated in several earlier works which date from just after 1500, such as the Palazzo Vendramin-Calergi and the churches of Santa Maria Domini and San Salvatore, these were all still fundamentally connected to long Venetian traditions. By about 1530, however, Venetian patrons, particularly the city government, were ready to accept a style based on non-Venetian traditions even for civic buildings in the heart of the Republic. For the first time a foreigner was able to introduce quite new elements into the city. The difference between the arcade of the Procuratie Vecchie (Plate 96) and the Library (Plate 99) indicates the change as perhaps no other example can. The Procuratie is in many important respects only an updating of a 12th-century Venetian form; the Library, on the other hand, is entirely Roman in spirit and form. It is the appearance of Sansovino's first Venetian works that marks the change from the Early to the High Renaissance in Venice.

The Plates

1 Piazza San Marco (see Fig. 17)
2 San Marco
3 Palazzo Ducale
4 Library of San Marco
5 San Michele in Isola
6 San Zaccaria
7 San Pietro di Castello
8 San Giovanni in Bragora
9 Santa Maria Formosa
10 Madonna dell'Orto
11 Ss. Giovanni e Paolo
12 San Giovanni Crisostomo
13 San Salvatore
14 Santa Maria dei Miracoli

15 Santa Maria Gloriosa dei Frari
16 San Fantino
17 Santa Maria dei Carmini
18 San Giobbe
19 Sant' Elena
20 San Giacomo dell'Orio
21 San Rocco
22 Santa Maria Mater Domini
23 San Sebastiano
24 San Giovanni Elemosinario
25 San Felice
26 San Giuliano
27 San Lio
28 Santi Apostoli

29 Cà d'Oro
30 Palazzo Bernardo
31 Cà del Duca
32 Cà Dario
33 Palazzo Pisani-Moretta
34 Palazzo Minelli
35 Palazzo Contarini degli Scrigni
36 Palazzo dell'Ambasciatore
37 Palazzo Morolin
38 Palazzo Zorzi a San Severo
39 Palazzo Gussoni
40 Campo San Silvestro
41 Palazzo Corner-Spinelli
42 Palazzo Manzoni-Angaran

43 Palazzo Vendramin-Calergi
44 Palazzo Contarini delle Figure
45 Palazzo Grimani a San Polo
46 Palazzo Grimani a San Luca
47 Scuola Grande di San Marco
48 Scuola Grande di San Giovanni Evangelista
49 Scuola Grande di San Rocco
50 San Giorgio Maggiore
51 Arsenale
52 Fondaco dei Tedeschi
53 Rialto: Fabbriche Vecchie
54 Palazzo dei Camerlenghi

Plate 1
MADONNA DELL'ORTO
Portal, 1460 (slightly reworked *c.* 1483). Bartolomeo Buon

The contract for the portal of the Madonna dell'Orto dates from 1460. Although the carving was close to completion in late 1461, the portal was not set in place until 1483. In some respects the work is a stylistic hybrid, as important changes were made at the time it was put in position.

Around the door itself are rope mouldings, braided columns and an outer frame in alternating courses of red and white marble that continues up over the doorway to form a semicircular tympanum. Flanking the doorway are two pedestals supporting free-standing columns with composite capitals. Above these, two octagonal pedestals carry an Annunciation group and the foliated reverse-curve moulding that forms the outer frame of the tympanum. On the pinnacle is a figure of St Christopher.

All of the elements of the portal are stylistically consistent with the date 1460 except for the fluted corona around the porphyry semicircle in the tympanum. There is nothing in Venice of this sort before Codussi's façade of San Michele in Isola (Plate 4), which was completed in 1478. By the time the Madonna dell'Orto portal was finally put in place it was already old-fashioned. It would have been impractical to replace it, but it does seem that it was, to some extent, brought up to date by modifying the design along the lines of San Michele in Isola. This 'modernization' resulted in the unusual combination of a late Gothic reverse-curve foliated moulding and a much more classicizing semicircular corona.

The contrast in both colour and material between the brick façade and the white stone of the portal and the circular window frame above it is quite characteristic of Venetian Gothic architecture; there are several churches in the city that show this treatment, such as the Frari, San Stefano and Ss. Giovanni e Paolo (Plate 2). The contrast between the courses of red and white marble was once much stronger; the red Verona marble used in Venice for this sort of decorative highlighting tends to fade slowly on exposure to weather.

Plate 2
Ss. GIOVANNI e PAOLO
Portal, 1459–63. Bartolomeo Buon

In the portal of Ss. Giovanni e Paolo, the recessed rectangular doorway is framed by full columns. The effect achieved by recessing the doorway and flanking columns and projecting the pairs of outer columns at each side under sections of entablature that break forward over them, is extremely bold and sculptural. The contrast between the thick column shafts and the slender rope and foliate colonnettes is heightened by the absence of capitals on the colonnettes. The columns and colonnettes support a continuous entablature with a complex shape: over the outer columns it projects, but it is straight; over the inner columns it is octagonal, more an extension of the column shafts than a horizontal element. Above the entablature rises a lightly pointed arch with a thick cylindrical moulding treated as a dense cluster of leaves, flowers and fruit. The line from the inner columns to the point of the arch is continuous, and has a fairly uniform diameter, but it changes texture and form four times in its rise from the smooth shaft to the leafy capital to the octagonal entablature and then to the leaf and fruit moulding.

The paired columns supporting a broken entablature with a vine-pattern decoration derive from the Arch of the Sergii in Pula (Fig. 1), which was also the source for the lower section of the Arsenale portal (Plate 70), but at Ss. Giovanni e Paolo the columns and entablature are still in an un-Classical relationship to the main arch. At the Arch of the Sergii and the Arsenale portal the columns and entablature frame the central arch at the sides and top; no major element of the ground storey rises above the entablature. At Ss. Giovanni e Paolo the main arch is above the entablature in a more medieval sequence.

The contrast between the portal of Ss. Giovanni e Paolo and Buon's contemporary portal of the Madonna dell'Orto (Plate 1) is striking; the interlocking of the elements of Ss. Giovanni e Paolo is much more imaginative, and the whole design more robust and inspired than the spidery forms of the Madonna dell'Orto.

The Ss. Giovanni e Paolo portal is characteristic of some of the most interesting architecture of the third quarter of the 15th century in its use of Classical elements to enliven the Gothic.

Plate 3
SAN ZACCARIA

Nave. Begun 1458 by Antonio Gambello; completed *c.* 1485 by Mauro Codussi

Gambello's nave of San Zaccaria is unusually tall for its length. The height is exaggerated by the elevation of the nave columns on very tall pedestals. The bases of the octagonal part of these pedestals (Fig. 4) are elaborately and quite strangely carved, and are unique in Venice.

The aisles of San Zaccaria are relatively narrow, and separating the groin-vaulted bays are pointed arches, a sharp contrast to the semicircular arches of the nave.

The wall system of round nave arches tangent to a strong entablature carried on brackets aligned with the nave columns, was first devised by Brunelleschi in the 1420s (Fig. 11). Codussi was probably responsible for the entablature and brackets, for it was he who changed the vault system of the nave, placing a dome over the third bay. The clerestory windows of the nave, also by Codussi, have tracery almost identical to the pattern of the façade windows of his Palazzo Corner-Spinelli (Plate 63).

There is a pronounced difference in scale between the nave and the choir, with its semioctagonal screen of columns and tracery. The ambulatory around the choir is appreciably lower than the aisles. This creates an odd join at the ends of the aisles where there is an expanse of wall between the round arches over the entrances to the ambulatory and the pointed arches over the aisles. While such passages seem at first to suggest a change in design or architect, they are not inconsistent with the deliberate and apparently original differences between the round and pointed arches of the nave and aisles, or the striking shift of scale and decoration between the nave and choir.

Plate 4
SAN MICHELE IN ISOLA
Façade, completed 1478. Mauro Codussi

In the façade of his first Venetian church Codussi made a number of major innovations. In the use of Istrian stone for the entire façade he departed from local tradition. There are, however, some churches in Venetian territory in the north-eastern Adriatic that may have provided the inspiration (Plate 10). It is clear that Codussi recognized the possibilities of Istrian stone for the façade of a church on a small island in the Venetian lagoon. White is used as a colour here and, set between the blue of the water and the sky, the façade is almost as impressive for its dazzling brightness as for its architectural organization.

Codussi effectively exploited the contrast between the white façade and the dark openings of the doorway and windows. These shapes were kept very simple, and the four strong contrasting areas are important elements of the design. Smaller dots of contrast appear in the upper areas; four porphyry and *verde antico* roundels frame the oculus while a fifth accent, an ellipse, is centred in the semicircular tympanum. Not all of the colour contrasts are strong, however; the cornices of the quadrant arches flanking the central field of the second storey, the central field itself and the semicircular pediment above it are edged with subtle, light blue-grey marble.

Codussi was extremely sensitive to texture, and the most remarkable aspect of the façade is the variety of textures kept in balance: the stone pattern of the lower storey, the shells in the quadrants, the veined marble around the oculus, the radial flutes of the corona of the tympanum. Even the Albertian frieze inscriptions, in handsome and correct ancient Roman lettering, the first of this type to be found in Venice, make a texture across what would otherwise be plain surfaces.

Codussi sought a system that would allow him to give the quadrant cornices the same profile as those of the first and second storeys, and to have their join with the pilasters of the central field correspond to the projection of the two entablatures over the pilasters they carry. This meant that the pilasters had to be cut in half, and their shafts are somewhat dwarfed by the quadrant cornices, but the façade is brilliantly coherent despite this not entirely successful passage. There was to be no Venetian church façade as intelligently organized as San Michele until the creation of Palladio's façades of San Francesco della Vigna and San Giorgio Maggiore in the mid-16th century.

Plate 5
SAN PIETRO DI CASTELLO
Bell Tower, 1482–8. Mauro Codussi

Although far from the centre of the city, San Pietro di Castello was the cathedral of Venice; San Marco was the Ducal palatine church and did not become the cathedral until 1810. Until the fall of the Venetian Republic in 1797, the government, ever on guard against Church power, kept the Patriarch of Venice at arm's length, in the corner of the city farthest from San Marco.

The San Pietro di Castello tower is free-standing, the usual arrangement for Italian cathedral towers. Venetian bell towers were usually built of brick; the San Pietro di Castello tower was the first of very few to be constructed in Istrian stone. While many towers in Venice were decorated with pilaster strips rising unbroken the entire height of the shaft (Plate 24), there were some, such as the ones at San Michele in Isola (Plate 18) and San Giobbe, completed in the 1460s, that were divided into two storeys by a horizontal element about half way up. Both must have been known to Codussi: the tower at San Michele was completed just before he arrived there to rebuild the abbey church, and San Giobbe was a centre of building activity in the 1460s and 1470s.

Above the first level of shaft flutes on the San Pietro di Castello tower is a strong cornice with dentil and egg-and-dart mouldings, but above the second level, just below the belfry, is a form which approximates a full Classical entablature, with an architrave, a blank frieze and a cornice. Codussi's attempt to balance the vertical sections with strongly accented horizontals indicates the new application of Classical ideas to a bell tower.

The tower was badly damaged by lightning in the 17th century and the original dome, known from the Jacopo dei Barbari view (Plate 19), was removed. The design of the top of the tower consisted of an open belfry, an octagonal drum with two arches on each face enclosed by a balustrade, and a dome. This is exactly the same system we find in the tower at San Michele in Isola, although there the decoration is still Gothic in style.

At San Pietro di Castello Codussi brought an established form up to date by changing Gothic vocabulary to Classical, and changing the material from brick to Istrian stone, while preserving the general organization of the earlier type. This is precisely what he had done in the façade of San Michele in Isola a decade earlier (Plate 4).

Plate 6
SAN ZACCARIA
Choir, begun *c.* 1460. Antonio Gambello

The choir of San Zaccaria is the most unusual part of the church, and by far the most difficult to date and attribute. We do not know how long it took to build; some details may have been subtly altered or brought up to date in the course of its construction. The capitals of the lower arcade are close in type to those at San Michele in Isola (Plate 15), but whether this means that Codussi had anything to do with the work at this level is difficult to determine. On the other hand, the tracery of the upper arches is not at all in the style of Codussi; it is very different from his tracery in the clerestory, and belongs instead to a style seen in palaces of the 1450s (Plate 54).

The elevation of the San Zaccaria choir is extremely coherent and integrated; with clusters of four ground-level columns arranged in a diamond pattern carrying arches on each side and colonnettes on both the interior of the choir and on the ambulatory (Plate 7), it has a more interesting wall-relief system than any Venetian architecture of the period. In the imaginative continuation of the verticals through two storeys, it recalls the portal of Ss. Giovanni e Paolo, which was also begun around 1460.

While there was no attempt to make the choir decoration relate to the nave, except by the continuation of the panelling of the nave bases around the base of the choir (Plates 3, 7), an attempt was made to relate the height of the choir entablature to the nave columns that abut it. While this alignment is not exact, it is quite close, and from some views (Plate 3), the columns against the piers seem to support the ends of the choir entablature.

The choir is a combination of Gothic and Classical forms that, although a bit more extreme, is similar to several examples from the period. Despite the unusual mixed vocabulary, some features can be related to Venetian traditions: the single arches of the lower level and the divided arches above preserve the rhythm of the Procuratie Vecchie; the combination of round arches on the lower level and pointed arches above was used in the east courtyard façade of the Palazzo Ducale in the 1480s (Plate 90).

Plate 7
SAN ZACCARIA
Ambulatory. Begun *c.* 1460 by Antonio Gambello; completed
c. 1490 by Mauro Codussi

The ambulatory of San Zaccaria is an unexpected element in a
Venetian convent church of the 15th century. It has been
suggested recently that it was built to accommodate the large
procession in the church during the annual Easter visit of the
Doge and the Signoria. This was an old and important custom
by the 1460s; its origins lie in the 12th century, when the nuns
of San Zaccaria gave a portion of their land to the Doge for the
enlargement of the Piazza San Marco. The Doge's procession
to the church was a yearly expression of gratitude, and its significance for the convent resulted in the creation of an elegant
architectural setting that would be appropriate for it.

There are striking differences in style and scale between the
semicircular chapels and the two-storey arcade around the
choir. The decoration of the chapels, with niches formed by
wall columns carrying undecorated arches, is derived from San
Marco. The choir arcade, on the other hand, is a combination
of Classical and Gothic elements.

The ground-storey columns of the choir arcade are cylindrical, with octagonal shafts above them, whereas on the chapel
side there are tall octagonal bases supporting cylindrical
columns; so there is a contrast at each level between the elements on opposite sides of the ambulatory. This sort of subtle
variety is characteristic of Venetian buildings of the later 15th
century, when architects seem to have been eager to avoid
tedious uniformity.

The building history of San Zaccaria is not completely clear,
and some parts of the ambulatory are difficult to assign to a
specific architect. If the choir arcade is probably attributable to
Gambello, the oval domes over the ambulatory must be credited
to Codussi, who was likely responsible as well for the decoration
of the radiating chapels.

Plate 8
SAN ZACCARIA
Façade. Begun 1458 by Antonio Gambello; completed
c. 1490 by Mauro Codussi

When Codussi took over at San Zaccaria in 1483 the façade
had progressed only as far as the lower storey. In the upper
levels Codussi rejected the rich colourism of Gambello's ground
storey in favour of Istrian stone. Only in the uppermost levels,
in the friezes of the top entablature and the pediment, did he use
coloured marble and polychrome inserts in any quantity.

Where the decorative corner elements of the projecting buttresses of Gambello's ground storey were very slender twisted
colonnettes stacked up three to a storey (Fig. 2), Codussi's
decoration is much larger in scale; on the third level of the
façade there are two tall free-standing columns at the corners
of each buttress. The row of shell niches on the second storey
of the façade is Codussi's inspired transition from Gambello's
ground storey to his own upper levels of the façade.

At San Michele in Isola, Codussi cut the pilasters of the
upper storey with the quadrant cornices but left the central
field open. At San Zaccaria he rethought the arrangement, and
decided to continue the quadrant cornices across the centre of
the façade as an unbroken horizontal, and divided what would
have been the central field into two low storeys, with pilasters
on one level and free-standing columns above. This system
prohibited a large oculus, but it had the virtue of avoiding the
sliced pilasters to which he had been forced at the other church.

There are many more openings in the façade of San Zaccaria
than there were at San Michele in Isola, and the contrasts of
simple shapes in the earlier church are nowhere to be seen;
although there are roundels in the quadrants and pediment of
San Zaccaria, they are lost in a proliferation of windows, niches,
columns and pilasters. San Zaccaria is a much taller church
than San Michele in Isola, and Codussi had no choice but to
divide it into three more storeys than the earlier work. The
system he used to accomplish this was a compromise: fascinat-
ing, extremely rational, at times brilliant, but not a complete
success in every respect.

Plate 9
SANTA MARIA FORMOSA
Nave, 1492–1504. Mauro Codussi

Santa Maria Formosa was altered in the 17th, 18th and 19th centuries, bombed in World War I and extensively rebuilt in the 1920s, but although several features of the building as it now stands, such as the fully developed east end and the drum under the crossing dome, are not original, the church still retains much of its late 15th-century character.

The space of Santa Maria Formosa is impressively organized, and its wide pyramidal effect is unusual for Venetian churches.

The interior decoration of the building is extremely spare; there is not a single carved capital in the church. The 'entablature' of the nave and transepts is radically reduced to narrow mouldings. What amount to the architrave and cornice are done in Istrian stone but the high 'frieze' between them is just stuccoed wall.

It is characteristic of Venetian architecture of these years that there was little concern for the proportions of the orders; architects in Venice seem to have begun in a very different way from the Florentines. At San Lorenzo in Florence, for example (Fig. 11), Brunelleschi's spatial effects were developed from the proportions of the orders; he began with a unit linked to the size of the columns and pilasters and then derived the plan and elevation from it. Codussi, on the other hand, began at Santa Maria Formosa with a particular combination of spaces in mind. These were organized in their own terms, and he did not care if it proved to be impossible to connect them all in a consistent and unified system of decoration; the pilasters and horizontal elements were stretched and shrunk to fit the space they had to fill. The spaces at Santa Maria Formosa might never have been developed by an architect who thought of the orders as the basic modules of architectural sequences. In 15th-century Venice there may be no building as logically developed as Brunelleschi's San Lorenzo but nowhere in contemporary Florence is there anything to rival the coherent combination of differently shaped spatial units of Codussi's Santa Maria Formosa.

Plate 10
MUGGIA CATHEDRAL
Façade, begun 1467

The Cathedral of Muggia is not generally considered in discussions of Venetian architecture of the 15th century since it is not located in Venice, but its position at the north end of the Istrian peninsula in an area that was Venetian territory by the 15th century makes the building an extremely interesting and informative one.

The church has a trilobed silhouette and a façade that is built entirely of the Istrian stone which is native to the area and which was extensively quarried for buildings in Venice. The architect gave some thought to the division between the storeys of the façade, but went no farther than separating the lobed upper section from the ground level by means of the straight, unbroken moulding on which the oculus seems to rest.

The strong contrast of the simple dark openings and the light stone reappears in the façade of San Michele in Isola (Plate 4) in very much the same arrangement that we see here. Codussi may have been aware of this church or some other similar Istrian example and used it as a point of departure for the façade at San Michele built only a few years after the Muggia façade was begun. There are, to be sure, elements that Codussi rejected, such as the reverse curve of the central section and the broad expanse of even and uniform white surface but, drawing on several traditions at once, he brought to San Michele an awareness of Classical vocabulary, Albertian ideas for the Tempio Malatestiana (Fig. 5) and such Venetian examples as the white stone façade of Muggia Cathedral to create a wholly new form.

Plate 11
SAN GIOVANNI IN BRAGORA
Façade, begun about 1475

Dedicated to St John the Baptist, this church has been known for centuries as San Giovanni in Bragora (or Bragola). The origins of the name are obscure; Venetian chroniclers have sought its roots in the local dialect words for market square (*bragola*) – perhaps derived from the Greek word *agora* – and for fishing (*bragolare*).

The façade of San Giovanni in Bragora represents a Venetian trilobed Gothic façade type which still exists in several slightly varied examples in the city itself and outlying Venetian territories. It was in fact begun just about the time the façade of San Michele in Isola (Plate 4) was being completed, but it shows no influence of Codussi's interest in applying Classical vocabulary to the older form; San Michele in Isola might never have been built for all the effect it had on this design.

The same basic elements that appear in the façade of the Cathedral of Muggia (Plate 10) and San Michele in Isola re-appear here: the central doorway with a lunette above it, the two flanking windows and the oculus above. The lateral door-ways under the tall windows are not original; as a general rule Venetian churches did not usually have more than a central doorway, and none of the other churches with façades of this sort, in Venice or outside, has lateral doors, which weaken the design.

Rather than divide the façade into horizontal registers, as was done somewhat tentatively at Muggia, the architect of San Giovanni in Bragora used projecting buttresses to divide the façade vertically into three strong and clear sections. The reverse curve of the central tympanum of the older Muggia type was rejected in favour of a uniform semicircle, but the shape of the pinnacle at the crown of the façade indicates a lingering fondness for a Gothic interplay of a variety of curves and angles.

Plate 12
SANTA MARIA DEI MIRACOLI
Façade and flank, 1481–9. Pietro Lombardo

The most lavishly decorated Venetian church of the late 15th century, Santa Maria dei Miracoli was built to house a miracle-working image of the Virgin and Child. In the first contract for the church Pietro was specifically commissioned to find the finest Greek, Carrara and Veronese marbles, *verde antico* and porphyry available. The church was paid for by public offerings to the image, and the rich treatment was intended to reflect the intensity of popular devotion.

With its simple rectangular nave and semicircular roof the church is often likened to a small coffer or reliquary, an appropriate conceit for a building to house a miraculous image.

Almost every field of the façade is filled with a decorative device of porphyry or *verde antico*. The undecorated fields of the façade and flanks are subdivided by strips of red, green or grey marble. Every window frame is carved with vine patterns, and in every spandrel of the upper storey is a half-length sculpted figure of a prophet.

Free-standing and fully revetted with marble, the Miracoli comes close to realizing Alberti's ideal of a city church, although in his name some critics have taken exception to parts of the building. Pietro wanted to have the main portal wider than the bays that flank it, which meant disrupting the rhythm of the arches on the storey above. This appears not to have bothered him, for his concern was first and foremost for rich effect, but it has often been singled out, unfairly, as evidence of incomprehension of Classical principles. A similar arrangement is known from other Venetian buildings of the 15th century, such as the Cà d'Oro (Fig. 15). Some purists have also been disturbed by the sequence of Corinthian capitals on the ground storey and Ionic above, the opposite of such authoritative antique buildings as the Colosseum in Rome, but clearly Pietro preferred to place the more interestingly carved capitals on a level where they could be seen rather than follow the orthodox Roman sequence. It is very characteristic of Venetian architecture of the later 15th century that, in a conflict between rich effect and Classical regulations, the tendency was to prefer the former. This attitude can be traced through the history of Venetian building to San Marco itself, where the decoration of the exterior is sumptuous and irrational.

Plate 13
PALAZZO DELL'AMBASCIATORE
c. 1455

The architectural elements of the Palazzo dell'Ambasciatore are very carefully arranged and scaled. The façade is organized in three storeys and three vertical sections with the central *piano nobile* section the most decorated. The whole is framed at the sides with very regular Istrian stone quoining with slender spiral colonnettes. Rope mouldings of two slightly different sizes separate the three storeys. There is a progression in the shapes and decoration of the windows from the low openings with segmented tops on the ground floor through the rectangular ones on the mezzanine to the taller ones in the two upper storeys,

a system almost identical to that of the Palazzo Pisani-Moretta (Plate 54).

The most unexpected feature of the façade of the Palazzo dell'Ambasciatore is the pair of shell niches between the flank windows of the *piano nobile* containing free-standing sculptures of shield-bearers. These niches are much larger than the ones at the Palazzo Bernardo (Plate 53), which contain only coats of arms. The niches may have been part of the original façade design, or added or enlarged some years later. The style of the present sculptures suggests the 1470s or 1480s, but we do not know if they replaced earlier sculptures in the niches. The idea of decorating palace façades with free-standing figure sculpture was never popular in Venice, and this example is exceptional in our period.

Plate 14
SAN GIOVANNI IN BRAGORA
Nave, begun 1475

San Giovanni in Bragora has a nave and flanking side aisles covered with an open timber roof. The nave roof is built with a combination of quadrant curves at its base and then a straight gable rising to a peak. This complex form is characteristic of one type of Venetian wooden roof of the 15th century, when a number of churches in Venice and on the mainland were covered with elaborate shapes, often called 'ship-bottom roofs' from their resemblance to the hull of a boat, that sometimes took on a form quite similar to that of the trilobed façade. There was not, however, always a direct connection between the façade shape and the form of the nave roof behind it.

The stuccoed brick walls have decorative bands painted around the pointed nave arches. This system is well known from Venetian churches of the early and mid-15th century, and here makes one of its last appearances in Venice.

The simple column shafts with their plain capitals were re-used from an earlier church on the site that was replaced in the building campaign of the 1470s and 1480s. The two nave arcade supports closest to the east end of the church are very different in style and proportion from the columns; they are richly carved square piers that rise from tall pedestals. With their decorated capitals and impost blocks they now seem oddly isolated, but as we see it today the church is quite different from the way it appeared in the late 15th century. In the 1490s a choir-screen was built which enclosed the last bay of the nave and high-altar chapel in a precinct separated from the rest of the church. The enclosing wall would have been as high as the pedestals of the nave piers. This choir lasted until the 17th century when it was replaced by the present high-altar chapel with its heavily stuccoed groin vault.

San Giovanni in Bragora indicates the strong but by no means unimaginative conservative current that ran through Venetian architecture of the last years of the 15th century. Although an architectural style more pregnant with the future had already made an appearance in the city, the vitality of the Venetian traditions was largely undiminished.

Plate 15
SAN MICHELE IN ISOLA
Nave, *c.* 1468–*c.* 1480. Mauro Codussi

In some respects the interior of San Michele in Isola is as radical a departure from tradition for a Venetian church as the façade, although not nearly so dramatic in appearance.

The most unusual feature of the five-bay interior is the flat ceiling of the nave and aisles. This appears to be the first such treatment of a Venetian church and probably has its source in earlier 15th-century Florentine churches such as Brunelleschi's San Lorenzo (Fig. 11) where, however, only the nave had a flat ceiling. The same round-headed 'Brunelleschian' windows found on the façade appear in the clerestory and aisles of the interior, also an unprecedented arrangement in Venice where windows were often more complex and not so uniform from one level to the next. There is no transept at San Michele; the dome is not over a crossing, as in the Brunelleschi churches, but over the high-altar chapel.

Although the aisles are covered in the same way as the nave, there is no attempt to extend the rhythm of the nave to the aisles. Similarly there was no attempt to tie the nave and choir together in a consistent proportional system. The richly carved chapel and the apse beyond it have a continuous entablature that does not correspond to any horizontal in the nave. This lack of integration, or deliberate separation of parts of the building through different decorative systems, is characteristic of several Venetian churches of the second half of the 15th century, and we find it at San Giobbe (Plate 25) and at San Zaccaria (Plate 6).

The round arches of the nave are not the first examples in Venice. Gambello's nave of San Zaccaria (Plate 3) has a round arcade, but the simple moulded bases of the columns and the open clarity of the San Michele interior are very different from San Zaccaria, and indicate that Codussi was sensitive to the spirit of Brunelleschi's innovations in Florence of a half-century before.

Plate 16
CA DARIO
c. 1488. Pietro Lombardo?

The Cà Dario is one of the most richly decorated palaces of the late 15th century. It was built for Giovanni Dario, Secretary of the Senate who, as Venetian representative, had concluded peace with the Turks in 1479. As a loyal servant of Venice Dario had the palace inscribed with a dedication to the city: URBIS GENIO IOANNES DARIUS is written under the four roundels on the lowest storey. Perhaps the dedication also served to avoid a charge of sumptuousness for Dario's personal indulgence – this is not the only example in this period of an inscription disclaiming personal glory for its owners (Plate 64).

The palace is often attributed to Pietro on the basis of the similarity of the revetment and some details to the decoration of the Santa Maria dei Miracoli façade (Plate 12).

The asymmetrical façade is fully revetted with marble; framed roundels of varying sizes fill up every available field. The largest decorative elements on the three upper storeys are framed by intertwining mouldings that were only rarely applied to palace façades. On the second storey, under the windows at the edges of the façade, are marble screens pierced in a manner similar to that of the side balcony of the Palazzo Morolin (Plate 58). Despite the richness of the surfaces and the pierced screens, there is no tracery in the windows; while the architect retained the Gothic idea of extensive surface decoration of palace façades, he rejected some of the Gothic means to achieve it.

The effect of the Cà Dario façade is often described as pictorial rather than architectural, the notion being that the design is conceived more for its richly coloured surfaces and its delight to the senses than for its organization of proportioned elements according to an intellectual system. That this style does to some degree deserve to be called pictorial is demonstrated by the fact that the closest similarities to it are found in the settings and background architecture of contemporary paintings, particularly those of Carpaccio, but the distinction between an architecture of rich and colouristic effect on the one hand, and an architecture of Classical proportion, harmony and sequence on the other, is not one that is likely to have occurred to a 15th-century Venetian. The idea that what appeals to the senses is less worthwhile than what appeals to the mind would have been totally foreign to Dario and his architect.

Plate 17
SAN MICHELE IN ISOLA
Monks' gallery, *c.* 1480

It is not uncommon in Venetian monastic churches for there to be an elevated gallery across the nave at some distance from the altar. These galleries are sometimes attached to the inner wall of the façade, as at Santa Maria dei Miracoli and San Sebastiano, or sometimes, as at San Michele, they are free-standing. This gallery, the first in Venice to be built in a clear Classical style, is placed in the second bay of the nave, creating a vestibule in the first bay and separating it from the rest of the church. The side toward the altar, seen here, has piers support-ing arches and applied half-columns on pedestals carrying an entablature which breaks forward over them. The garland swags around the half-columns are unknown in Venice before this time. The section above the entablature is treated as the attic of a Roman arch. The strongly veined marble at this level, and in the spandrels on the level below, is the only concession to traditional Venetian taste for rich material.

The San Michele gallery makes an interesting contrast to the Frari choir-screen of only a few years earlier (Plate 20). The difference, to be seen in many details, is particularly apparent in the entablatures; while these both break forward lightly over the capitals which carry them, they have little else in common. The Frari screen has an entablature (not including the inscribed cornice above it), with a dense leafy pattern that is late Gothic in style; at San Michele all of the entablature elements are Classical, from the fascia of the architrave to the dentil and egg-and-dart cornice.

Plate 18
SAN MICHELE IN ISOLA
Bell Tower, *c.* 1465

Plate 19
VIEW OF VENICE Jacopo dei Barbari
1500. Detail showing the original appearance of the Bell
Tower of San Pietro di Castello. (See Plate 5.)

Plate 20
SANTA MARIA GLORIOSA DEI FRARI
Choir-screen, begun *c.* 1460, completed 1475

The Frari choir-screen was built to close off the area where the
monks worshipped from the rest of the church. Its rich decoration on the nave side is secondary to its main purpose, although
it was provided with pulpits facing the nave for preaching to
the laity.

The date 1475 appears in an inscription; this is probably the
date of the completion of the screen. There is only stylistic
evidence for dating the start of work on the project, and for the
identification of the artists who designed and executed it. As
the sculptural style of some of the panels with half-length
figures is close to the work of Pietro Lombardo, a prominent
role is often assigned to him, but while he may have finished the
screen, he certainly did not begin it, and he may have worked
on it only as a sculptor.

The style of the architectural decoration is an interesting
mixture, but with the exception of the clear Roman lettering of
the inscription, it is almost entirely late Gothic. The profile
of the base closely resembles the base of the San Zaccaria
façade (Fig. 2), which dates from the late 1450s. The heavy
foliage of the consoles under the pulpits and on the capitals
shows no Classical influence at all, and maintains a style that
had been in fashion in Venice since the 1430s. Some aspects of
the pilaster decoration, on the other hand, such as the leafy
tendrils that grow from urns, indicate the same interest in this
kind of Classical form that we see around 1460 in the entablature of the Ss. Giovanni e Paolo portal (Plate 2). In the Frari
screen the thick, juicy leaves are still Gothic in spirit, and the
treatment is very different from the carving at San Giobbe
(Plates 25, 26), which represents the style more accurately associated with Pietro in the early 1470s.

The way the inscribed frieze rests on top of an element older
in style suggests that the inscription was added when the work
was finished, but was not part of the original design. An inscription similar in its lettering style is found on the façade of
San Michele in Isola (Plate 4). This must date from around
1475 and might have been the source for the one on the Frari
screen.

Plates 21, 22
SANTA MARIA DEI CARMINI
Choir, and Aisle apse, *c.* 1505–11. Sebastiano da Lugano

The reconstruction of the choir and the aisle apses of Santa Maria dei Carmini is one of the more curious Venetian works of the early 16th century. The structural system of the new parts of the church, with its four-part rib vault over the high altar and its strongly sectioned rib vaults in the central and aisle apses, is Gothic, but the decorative vocabulary is largely Classical. An attempt was made, in an interesting and not always consistent way, to respect the proportions of Classical architectural forms in a non-Classical structural system. Framing the opening into the choir are engaged piers with fluted capitals now partly obscured by the organ- and choir-lofts. These piers support a complete Classical entablature that runs along the walls of the choir and aisle chapels and around the apses. Above this level in the choir there is a low storey terminated by a cornice which also continues completely around the apse. These two horizontal elements divide the choir apse windows into three sections. Above two levels of rectangular openings is a ring of even semicircular lights with a blank wall space above them and a ribbed apse vault. This part of the church is very bright, and its closest parallel in Venetian architecture is to be found in 14th-century churches; in the 15th century no choir apse was so glazed.

In the aisle chapels the elevation is one storey lower than in choir and the semicircular windows are eliminated. Clearly visible in Plate 22 is the architect's attempt to utilize Classical forms: the pilasters which support the arch separating the aisle from its apse are given composite or Ionic capitals and moulded edges. These pilasters carry an entablature which has some orthodox Classical details (such as a dentil moulding in the cornice) but also some moulding profiles that are very unusual. From this entablature rise the ribs of the pointed-arch apse vault. The angled piers between the apse windows are carved to create in the crease between them a colonnette of the same diameter as the vault ribs, but while the vault ribs are the continuation of these colonnettes, the transition from one level to the next is nonetheless very abrupt.

Fusions of Gothic and Classical systems are not unknown in earlier Venetian architecture, as we know from the choir of San Zaccaria (Plate 6) and the courtyard façade of the east wing of the Palazzo Ducale (Plate 90), but it is a bit surprising to find the impulse to combine the two styles persisting in a work as late as this. Apparently the architect felt that the church should retain something of the Gothic spirit of its nave in the new east end, but at the same time he wished to bring the vocabulary up to date. The attempt made at Santa Maria dei Carmini to bring these two contrasting styles into some sort of harmony appears to have been the last such effort in Venice.

Plate 23
SAN GIACOMO DELL'ORIO
High-altar chapel, *c.* 1498

In the last years of the 15th century the old Gothic choir of San Giacomo was removed and replaced by one with a barrel vault and apse. Two windows placed close to the sides of the apse light the choir. The style of the carving on the tall pedestals, the pilaster capitals, the entablature that continues around the apse, and the two arches under the barrel vault, have suggested to some scholars that either Pietro Lombardo or one of his sons worked here. However, the form of the San Giacomo choir – even in many of its details – is taken over almost without change from the Chapel of the Holy Cross at San Michele in Isola. This chapel, designed by Codussi, was finished by the early 1480s. The similarity between the two works extends to many of the details: there is a very similar treatment of the arches of the barrel vaults, which have the same fluting, the same number of panels on their undersides and almost identical rosettes in the panels. The Chapel of the Holy Cross was almost certainly the source for the San Giacomo choir, but the similarity between the two is not in itself sufficient to argue for the attribution of the San Giacomo choir to Codussi, for anyone could have copied his earlier chapel.

The new San Giacomo choir makes no concessions whatsoever to the style of the earlier nave. The striking contrast between the wooden ship-bottom roof of the nave and the stuccoed semicircular vault of the choir, as well as the abrupt change from the low nave supports to the much taller pilasters of the choir, indicate that the primary intention was to have the choir separate and distinct from the rest of the building, a very different approach from the one taken by the architect of the choir of Santa Maria dei Carmini.

Plate 24
SAN GIOBBE
Nave, c. 1460–c. 1470

San Giobbe was an active monastery in the 1450s and 1460s. San Bernardino of Siena had preached there in the 1440s. His friend Cristoforo Moro, an important Venetian nobleman who became Doge in 1462, was the major patron of the church in the 1450s and 1460s, and is buried beneath the high-altar dome.

The single nave of San Giobbe has a row of chapels opening off the left side and a row of altars down the right wall. A square altar chapel at the east end of the church, with a monks' choir behind it, is flanked by two shallow chapel apses.

The architect has not tried to create the rhythms or scaled sequences we customarily associate with important architecture. There is no concern to divide the single, wide space into smaller units; the chapels vary in size and form, and establish no pattern. The nave of San Giobbe is just a big room, and like many rooms it is made interesting by the things that are in it.

The most striking aspect of the San Giobbe nave, and perhaps its most influential, is its brightness. Its plain white stuccoed walls and white Istrian stone decoration were to reappear often in later Venetian churches such as Santa Maria Formosa and San Felice; but the influence of San Giobbe was not limited to the churches of the later 15th and early 16th centuries: perhaps the bright interiors of Palladio's San Giorgio Maggiore of the 1560s and Longhena's Santa Maria della Salute of the 1630s owe something to San Giobbe.

Plate 25
SAN GIOBBE
High-altar chapel, *c.* 1472. Pietro Lombardo

The high-altar chapel and the flanking chapel niches of San Giobbe are the first places in which we can observe several elements which were to become important in Venetian architecture in the next half century.

On the underside of the arch which spans the entrance to the main chapel are thirteen carved panels with the Agnus Deii in the centre and six apostles on each side. In style these are quite close to some of the prophet panels on the Frari choir-screen (Plate 20) and to Pietro's documented later work; on the basis of this similarity, both works are often attributed to or at least connected with him. Pietro was in Padua from about 1466 to 1470, and so the work at San Giobbe, which dates from 1472 and after, was probably among his first in Venice.

The pilaster decoration of vine and tendril patterns with urns, leaves, flowers and birds, is an antique style that was being revived in several places, including Urbino and Padua, at about this time. The light and graceful patterns are quite different from the thicker and heavier forms on the pilasters of the Frari choir-screen. The style of architectural decoration of San Giobbe was to be a major aspect of Pietro's later work, and was given its richest statement in the mid-1480s at Santa Maria dei Miracoli (Plate 29).

The pierced base of the high-altar chapel dome indicates a new look at Byzantine architecture, particularly San Marco (Fig. 8), but some other elements of the decorative programme here might also be regarded as evidence of a Byzantine revival. In the pendentives are roundels with the four evangelists. These are quite common in pendentives, but the *putti* beneath them at San Giobbe are not. In the pendentive mosaics of the central dome at San Marco there are angels under the four evangelists, and these may have suggested the *putti* to Pietro.

It may be that the evocation of San Marco by the type of dome and the *putti* under the evangelists was due to the fact that a Doge had chosen to be buried under the dome. San Marco was the Doge's church and it is not difficult to imagine that an architect might choose to design the dome over a Doge's tomb in a way that recalls the great basilica.

Plate 26
SAN GIOBBE
Portal, *c.* 1474. Pietro Lombardo

The portal of San Giobbe is a very representative example of the decorative style of Pietro. The pilasters of the doorway are extensively carved with classicizing tendril patterns that are mirror images of each other. These pilasters carry a full entablature with a frieze richly carved with palmettes. Enclosed by the pilasters and entablature is a door frame treated like an architrave, and similar to the architrave directly above it. The main entablature carries a semicircular pediment with a heavily decorated cornice. This style of doorway is Florentine in origin, and was perhaps brought to Venice by Pietro himself, who seems to have had some Florentine experience in the early 1460s. But if the general arrangement of a semicircular pediment over an entablature is in fact Tuscan in origin, it has already begun to show many non-Florentine elements, above all in the great proliferation across its surface of decorative carving. In Florence the pilasters would have been decorated only with fluting. In the pediment are low-relief figures of St Francis of Assisi and (St) Job. (In Venice several Old Testament figures are regarded as saints, and have churches dedicated to them: others include St Moses, St Jeremiah, St Daniel and St Samuel. This is common in Byzantium and is another example of eastern influence on Venice.)

On the ends of the entablature and the crown of the pediment are sculptures of Sts Louis, Anthony and Bernardino of Siena. The placement of sculptures at these points, which seems to have been done here for the first time, was to become a standard part of the Venetian style in the following years, and is to be found not only on doorways, but on church and *scuola* façades as well, as may be seen at Santa Maria dei Miracoli (Plate 12), San Zaccaria (Plate 8) and the Scuola San Marco (Plate 66).

Plate 27
SANT'ELENA
Portal, with Monument to Vettor Capello, *c.* 1475. Antonio
Rizzo

Carved in the same years as the portal of San Giobbe (Plate 26),
the portal of Sant'Elena offers a very interesting and instructive
contrast to it, for while obviously similar in some important
respects, the two portals represent different approaches to
architectural forms taken by two men trained as sculptors.

At Sant'Elena two fully round fluted columns with strong
composite capitals rise from pedestals to carry a heavily carved
cornice, supported also by brackets, that breaks forward in the
centre. This carries a similarly carved semicircular cornice.
Framing the door itself is a twisted moulding that is very close
in style to those found at the Madonna dell'Orto (Plate 1) and
Ss. Giovanni e Paolo (Plate 2), and may well belong to an earlier
building phase. In the lunette over the doorway is the monument to Vettor Capello, who died in 1467 fighting the Turks.
The hero kneels before St Helen, the mother of the Roman
emperor Constantine and the patroness of the church. Behind
the figures is a cenotaph, a purely symbolic sarcophagus;
Capello's body was buried elsewhere.

Tombs and monuments were common inside churches, and
wall tombs were sometimes built around or over doorways, but
the placement of such a monument on a façade portal is extremely unusual, and the reasons for it are unknown. Sant'Elena
has a rather large space in front of it, and the façade can be seen
from some way off. It has been suggested that this may have had
something to do with the decision to put the monument there.

The proportions of the pilasters and the entablature of the
San Giobbe portal are more in accordance with antique canons
than those of Sant'Elena (which lacks a full entablature), but
compared to the Sant'Elena portal the forms at San Giobbe
are flat and unemphatic; in the 1470s Pietro looked to the
surface decoration of antique architecture while Rizzo looked
to its monumental qualities.

Plate 28
SANTA MARIA DEI MIRACOLI
Exterior of east end, 1481–9

The east end of Santa Maria dei Miracoli shows several features that are unique in Venetian architecture of the late 15th century. The square high-altar chapel is attached to a rectangular nave, and in the angle between them is a bell tower. Three sides of this octagonal bell tower are absorbed into the body of the building; the tower shaft is revetted with the same marble used on the rest of the exterior, and the main horizontal elements of the nave and high-altar chapel extend around the tower, wedding the church and tower more tightly than in any other example in Venice.

The ground floor of the high-altar chapel is a sacristy lit by two windows on the canal side. Above it is the chapel proper, lit by round-headed windows similar to those in the nave. The pendentive zone of the interior is marked by the block beneath the drum and dome. A certain amount of fudging was required to fit the round window and the semicircular cornice on the canal side of this level behind the tower shaft, as well as to fit the open belfry into the main dome. The eccentric placement of the windows in their bays on the end wall of the high-altar chapel and at the end of the nave flank was necessary to accommodate the wall thickness which determined the window placement on the interior; the windows are up against the walls on the inside (see Plate 29).

The curious combination of a simple nave and a complex, multi-storied high-altar chapel most likely reflects the change in plan when it was decided to expand the Santa Maria dei Miracoli project from a votive chapel to house a miraculous image to a convent. A church required a more important and elaborate east end than a chapel, and it may have been because of the new need, combined with very limited space, that the high-altar chapel was raised over a ground-floor sacristy and these two spaces connected by the spiral staircase in the bell tower.

Plate 29
SANTA MARIA DEI MIRACOLI
Interior 1481–9. Pietro Lombardo

Plate 30
SAN MARCO
Mascoli Chapel, *c.* 1430

There is evidence in the documents dealing with the construction of the Miracoli that the first project was to be a votive chapel to house a miracle-working image. Only around 1485, when money from public donations continued to pour into the project treasury, was the decision made to build a convent church. It was with this change in plans that a wooden nuns' gallery across the façade end of the nave (from which Plate 29 was taken), and the elevated east end, were built. In his first contract Pietro was not indicated as the architect of the project, only as the man responsible for its construction, but in the second, when the building is specifically referred to as a church rather than a chapel, it is clearly stated that Pietro himself designed the east end.

That the project was originally to be a chapel is also suggested by the architectural sources of the interior, which are in a local chapel tradition. The single-aisle barrel-vaulted space is rare for churches, but it is known from the early 14th-century Scrovegni (Arena) Chapel in Padua, and the 15th-century Mascoli Chapel in San Marco. The Mascoli Chapel is also important for the Miracoli as the source for the system of marble wall revetment, and in both works the pictorial decoration is in the barrel vaults rather than on the walls – at the Miracoli there are fifty painted panels in the wooden ceiling.

Originally the upper level of the nave walls, in the area around the windows, was not revetted with marble, but most likely only decorated with stucco painted to look like marble. The end wall and the choir were revetted in marble from the start. The later application of the marble revetment in the window zone of the nave buried the window frames beneath the level of the marble, and required that niches be cut in the revetment to fit around the consoles that support the ceiling. The marble sheathing was probably added to the nave walls when the administrators of the Miracoli project found they had enough money from public contributors to pay for it.

The join of the nave and elevated east end is not entirely successful on the interior, just as it was not on the exterior. This is most evident in the awkward way the curve of the arch over the choir meets the curve of the barrel vault of the nave, which appears to be the result of a compromise necessitated by the two-stage building history.

The Miracoli choir is extensively carved, and the nave walls are completely covered with marble revetment; the interior is one of the richest in Venice after San Marco.

The east end of the church, with the hanging octagonal pulpits at the outer edges of the upper area, and access to the choir through the centre of the raised platform, recall the distribution of elements in the choir-screen of the Frari (Plate 20), on which Pietro probably worked. He appears to have had that earlier work in mind when he designed the Miracoli choir.

Plate 31
SANTA MARIA FORMOSA
North aisle and chapels, 1492–1504. Mauro Codussi

Codussi was extremely sensitive to the ways in which different types of vaulting could be employed, and at Santa Maria Formosa he worked out a rational system in which each part of the building is vaulted according to the role it plays in the plan of the church and the development of its interior space (Fig. 10). The groin-vaulted nave is tall and strongly longitudinal (Plate 9), while the barrel-vaulted chapels off the aisles are low and transverse. The shift of axis necessary to make the transition from one part to the other is achieved effectively in the aisle domes, which function equally on the longitudinal and the transverse axes.

Codussi's choice of domes on pendentives to cover the aisles was a very interesting one. In Brunelleschi's churches of San Lorenzo (Fig. 11) and Santo Spirito in Florence the aisles are covered with pendentive domes (a structure in which the spherical surface of the pendentives is continuous with that of the dome). Codussi chose instead to use domes on pendentives (a system found in San Marco and many other Venetian churches, in which the hemispherical dome rests on four pendentives that make the transition from the square bay to the inscribed circle which is the base of the dome). A dome on pendentives is higher than a pendentive dome and, to judge from the way the rest of the nave design is organized, it seems most likely that Codussi wanted the higher spaces at this point to strengthen the distinction between the aisles and the chapels

that extend transversally from them.

The way in which the spaces of the church, from the nave to the aisle chapels, are increasingly subdivided is striking. The bays of the nave vaults are not separated from one another by transverse arches (Plate 9), so that despite the fact that the nave is three bays long, it tends to be understood as a single unified space. The bays of the aisles, on the other hand, are separated by transverse arches, and the domes over each aisle bay are more distinct from each other than are the vaults of the nave bays. The transverse chapels which open off the aisles are divided from one another even more emphatically than are the aisle bays, and while the walls between them are pierced by a pair of low arches, the spaces are nevertheless very separate. The change from low, transverse and separate units to a tall, longitudinal and essentially single unit is one of the most interesting and effective sequences to be found in Venetian architecture of any period.

As a result of its wide, pyramidally arranged spaces, the interior of Santa Maria Formosa offers a great number of varying views as the visitor moves through it. The views from the nave into the aisles and the chapels and through the openings between the chapels, shift and realign constantly in an extremely interesting sequence. The domes over the aisles have no axes and appear the same from any angle but the elements around them change their appearance with every step the visitor takes. Perhaps only Codussi's own work at the ambulatory of San Zaccaria (Plate 6) or the staircase of the Scuola San Giovanni Evangelista (Plates 67, 84) can offer an architectural experience to rival that of walking through Santa Maria Formosa.

Plate 32
VIEW OF VENICE Jacopo dei Barbari, 1500
Detail showing original San Rocco façade

Plate 33
SAN ROCCO
Interior. Choir and flanking chapels, begun *c.* 1485.
Bartolomeo Bono

The church of San Rocco was begun in the mid-1480s, but radically changed in the 18th century. Of the original church only the east wall remains, with its high-altar chapel and lower flanking chapels. San Rocco is the first known work in Venice by Bono, who was active until his death in 1529, serving as *proto* of the Procurators of San Marco from 1505.

The east end of San Rocco is a development of the system of San Giobbe. While at San Giobbe the chapels flanking the high altar are only shallow niches covered with half-domes, at San Rocco they have been deepened and covered with groin vaults, although they still end in semicircular apses and half-domes. Another major change from the San Giobbe system is the insertion of a windowed drum between the pendentives and the dome of the high-altar chapel. This is to be seen also at Santa Maria dei Miracoli, under construction in the same years.

At San Rocco there are rosettes in the arches and the capitals are carved, but the rich decoration of the San Giobbe chapel arch and pilasters is eliminated. It is apparent from this that architecture and decoration were not regarded as necessarily connected: similar forms could range from plain to lavish.

The architect tried to organize the elevation of the east end so that the arches of the side chapels would rise from the level of the lower entablature of the choir. This required that the upper entablature and the arch of the central chapel be carried by a short second storey of piers. The result is awkward, and the arrangement was not taken up again, but it is an interesting indication of a desire to link the three eastern chapels more closely than they were at San Giobbe.

The façade of San Rocco was torn down in the 18th century, but its appearance is known from a number of prints. It was a variation of the lobed façade type found in such works as the Scuola San Marco (Plate 66) and the dormitory of San Giorgio Maggiore (Plate 78).

Plate 34
SAN SEBASTIANO
Nave, begun 1508. Antonio Scarpagnino

Much of the original character of San Sebastiano was altered in the later 16th century when the interior was extensively re-decorated. A heavy carved ceiling was added, and the walls and ceilings were painted by Paolo Veronese. As a single-nave church with a tall choir and lower flanking chapels on either side, San Sebastiano belongs to the same family of churches as San Giobbe and San Rocco. This type of church was to be an important influence later in the 16th century, for it served as the model for Sansovino's churches of San Giuliano (Fig. 14) and San Martino di Castello.

At San Sebastiano the system of the east-end chapels was made more regular and rational than it had been at San Rocco (Plate 33). In the earlier church the side chapels have groin vaults and apses with half-domes; at San Sebastiano they are covered with barrel vaults and end in flat walls rather than apses. The attempt made to link the main and flanking chapels at San Rocco was abandoned in favour of the system of San Giobbe, with the side-chapel arches rising from their own piers, lower than those which carry the main chapel. San Sebastiano does follow San Rocco in the suppression of almost all sculptural decoration; not even the undersides of the chapel arches are given carved decoration.

Plate 35
SAN SEBASTIANO
Façade, 1540s. Antonio Scarpagnino

The façade of San Sebastiano is in many respects not an entirely successful work, but it is interesting as an attempt on the part of the architect to introduce a number of new elements into Venetian church façade design. Several of the features of this façade appear to derive from palace architecture, and there is an analogy here to Codussi's use of palace façade details at San Michele in Isola (Plate 4), but the result is not as well integrated or effective. It may also be that Scarpagnino knew of recent developments in Roman architecture to which in some respects this design is related.

A very curious feature is the appearance of paired columns on a single projecting pedestal at the edges of the façade. Paired columns do appear on the façade of San Zaccaria (Plate 8) and in the façade of Palazzo Vendramin-Calergi (Plate 64), but at San Sebastiano they seem almost to have been used because they were available rather than for any reason of design coherence. The upper-storey columns are shorter than those below and, to make the two storeys the same height, the upper columns are raised on pedestals that create a disjuncture of scale between the columns and the windows next to them.

While segmental and triangular pediments had often been placed over church portals, at San Sebastiano we see the first attempt to top façade windows, usually simple openings, with pediments of both types. Pedimented windows are found in *scuole* (Plate 66), and on many palaces of the early 16th century (Plate 68), as well as in civic buildings (Plates 90, 91). The ribboned frames between the ground-storey columns are also unknown on church façades, but are part of a palace tradition, both private (Plate 68) and civic (Plate 90).

On the second storey the architect tried to achieve a transition from the plane of the wall to the plane of the projecting entablature above the columns by placing heavy segmental pediments over the lighter window frames, and a large bracket above the oculus. The result is rather awkward and the general impression of the San Sebastiano façade suggests an architect who was not entirely sure how to deal with the vocabulary he employed here. The San Sebastiano façade does reveal clearly that the kind of experimentalism that characterized the years between 1460 and the 1520s was still a force, albeit a minor one, as late as the 1540s.

Plate 36
SAN GIOVANNI CRISOSTOMO
Façade, begun 1497. Mauro Codussi

The San Giovanni Crisostomo façade is Codussi's simplest. The rich carved detail of his earlier façades has been dramatically reduced and the walls are stuccoed brick. It is possible that Codussi was reacting against his own earlier heavily decorated façades of San Michele in Isola (Plate 4) and San Zaccaria (Plate 8) by making everything much plainer. It must be borne in mind, however, that San Giovanni Crisostomo is on a very narrow street and can be seen from only a sharp angle; San Michele in Isola and San Zaccaria both rise in open areas that allow them to be seen in their totality from directly in front.

The organization of the San Giovanni Crisostomo façade is identical to that of San Michele in Isola. In both there is a central portal with a triangular pediment, round-headed windows on each side of it, and quadrants on the second level which frame a central section crowned with a semicircular pediment. The elements of the portal itself are much fuller at San Giovanni Crisostomo than at San Michele; Codussi clearly felt that the strong Istrian stone pattern of the San Michele façade would not allow such a heavy door frame, while the very plain surface of the San Giovanni Crisostomo façade required some strong relief.

At San Giovanni Crisostomo Codussi made the cornices of the quadrants slice across the pilasters of the central section, as they do at San Michele. While the treatment of the quadrant cornices is simpler than at San Michele, the solution is just as much an awkward compromise. Codussi seems to have been the only architect prepared to deal with the problem in this way; later architects avoided it, and San Giovanni Crisostomo is the last church in which we see this arrangement.

Plates 37, 38
SAN GIOVANNI CRISOSTOMO
Begun 1497. Present interior, and interior with reconstruction
of original choir vault. Mauro Codussi

The choir of San Giovanni Crisostomo was changed in the
17th century when the original barrel vault was replaced by a
flat ceiling so that windows could be cut into the upper walls
(Plate 37). This change seriously vitiated the effect of Codussi's
interior, which is reconstructed in Plate 38.

The elements of the architectural orders at San Giovanni
Crisostomo are more complete than they were at Santa Maria
Formosa (Plate 9); in this church there are Corinthian capitals
on the pilasters which carry the main entablature. This entablature is now full, with an Istrian stone frieze, and does not give
the impression, as it does at Santa Maria Formosa, of being just
a vestigial trace of an architectural form.

This church shows a much greater unity in its vaulting types
than Santa Maria Formosa; the groin vaults that appear in the
earlier church are gone (Fig. 12). In the corners between the
barrel-vaulted arms of San Giovanni Crisostomo are small
pendentive domes, and over the crossing is a full dome on
pendentives. The San Giovanni interior is also much more
vertical than Santa Maria Formosa, and Codussi shows a
sensitivity to the ordering of rising shapes that is as subtle as
was his treatment of spreading shapes at Santa Maria Formosa.
As Codussi had made the wide Santa Maria Formosa seem even

wider by his treatment of its elements, here he makes the
verticals more emphatic by raising the nave piers on tall pedestals. In the tightly clustered spatial units of San Giovanni
Crisostomo there is no change of axis from the sides to the
centre of the church; the domed corners are higher in proportion to the crossing than are the aisles of Santa Maria Formosa,
and none of the elements is read as having a predominantly
horizontal axis. The increasing domical reach of the two types,
pendentive domes in the corners and a dome on pendentives
in the centre, is brilliantly effective in its organization. The
imaginative way in which the domically lower forms are actually
placed at a lower level than the fully hemispherical central
dome indicates Codussi's sensitivity to vaulting forms was
perhaps even more refined here than it had been at Santa Maria
Formosa. The placement of pendentive domes in the corner
bays from which the central pendentives rise makes the two
pendentive forms overlap in the angled view of these bays
(Plate 38).

The experience of San Giovanni Crisostomo is very different
from that of Santa Maria Formosa. Movement through the
church to see steadily changing views is much less important
at San Giovanni Crisostomo than at the earlier church (Plate
31). The bold simplification of the shapes at San Giovanni
Crisostomo was accompanied by Codussi's increasing subtlety
in the handling of them, making the building a fitting climax
to his career as a church architect.

Plates 39, 40
SANTA MARIA MATER DOMINI
Nave and choir, begun 1504

In 1580 Francesco Sansovino described the interior of Santa
Maria Mater Domini as having been rebuilt in the early 16th
century on the pattern of the central 'cube' of San Marco, but
this church, with its two-bay nave and niche chapels flanking
the choir, is in fact much less like San Marco than is San Giovanni Crisostomo. There is, to be sure, a central dome on
pendentives, but the church is not as centralized as San
Giovanni Crisostomo, for the nave is two bays long and treated
in a quite different way from the transepts. The nave and choir
are groin-vaulted, and the transepts barrel-vaulted. This
probably has less to do with an interest in a variety of vaulting
than with the practical need to light the interior. The decision
to put windows high up in the nave walls made a groin vault
necessary; barrel vaults were practical only in the transepts,
where there are no windows.

The large three-part semicircular nave windows are not
original. Called 'thermal' windows because their form is derived
from windows in Roman baths (*thermae*), they do not appear in
Venice until the third quarter of the 16th century in the work of
Andrea Palladio. The nave windows of Santa Maria Mater
Domini date from the mid-17th century when, according to the
sources, 'small round windows', probably like the ones in the
nave of Santa Maria Formosa (Plate 9), were replaced.

The wall system of piers carrying arches and applied half-
columns carrying the nave entablature requires either a strongly
projecting straight entablature or one, as here, that breaks
forward over the capitals. A transverse arch over the nave
divides the vault into two bays, continuing the system of nave
arcade division by columns all the way up across the vaults.
While such an arrangement is already present at San Giovanni
Crisostomo, here it is more fully organized.

In the corners between the side walls and ends of the transepts, quarter-columns carry the entablature. This concern for
the logical and consistent application of the orders is new, and in
interesting contrast to San Giovanni Crisostomo, for example,
where in the corner of the transept (Plate 38) there is nothing
but the pilaster that carries the arch of the adjacent chapel,
and the entablature floats unsupported at this point. At Santa
Maria Mater Domini the transept corner columns carry an
arch that strongly marks off the flat semicircular end wall from
the barrel vault, making the divisions of the interior more consistent and emphatic than they had been in earlier churches.

Flanking the choir of Santa Maria Mater Domini (Plate 40)
and in line with the aisles, are two semicircular apsed niches
that recall the flanking chapels at San Giobbe (Plate 25), but
which are used in a different way. The corner domes of the San
Marco plan are to some extent illusionistically implied by the
clever and unusual treatment of the choir walls, which have
blind arches that roughly match the arches over the transept
niches. When seen in a strongly foreshortened view from the
nave, the choir walls and the niches combine to create the false
impression that there are actually domed bays at these corners
as there are, for example, at San Giovanni Crisostomo.

Santa Maria Mater Domini is unique among Venetian
churches of this period in that while it does not actually imitate
San Marco or other more fully centralized churches, it appears
to refer to them in several aspects of its design. The anonymous
architect could not, or did not wish to, build a central-plan
church, but he continued to imply one in the arrangement of the
transept niches and choir walls. In this respect the church is
very different from Santa Maria Formosa, for example, where
Codussi created an interior that contains no such references to
other buildings. In some respects Santa Maria Mater Domini
seems to be an attempt to combine the forms of Santa Maria
Formosa with the associations of San Giovanni Crisostomo.

Plate 41
SANTA MARIA MATER DOMINI
Façade, *c.* 1535

In the façade of Santa Maria Mater Domini the system of quadrants over the aisles, which Codussi often used to make the transition from the one-storey aisles to the two-storey nave (Plates 4, 36), was completely abandoned. Instead we find large volutes which rise in a concave rather than convex silhouette from the main entablature over the ground storey to the sides of the upper section. The pediment over the central upper section of the façade is now triangular. While there were other churches in Venice with triangular pediments on the façade (Plate 45), at Santa Maria Mater Domini we find for the first time the combination of such a pediment and flanking volutes. Henceforth there were to be no more façades in Venice of the trilobed kind that had been the dominant form for sixty years. The Santa Maria Mater Domini façade reveals the change of style that resulted from the arrival of Sansovino in Venice in the late 1520s, for it is a type with which architects in Florence and more especially in Rome had experimented in the early 16th century.

The elements of the Santa Maria Mater Domini façade are much more regular than those of the Venetian churches of Codussi and his followers. The aisle windows are rectangular rather than round-headed, and are topped by horizontal cornices placed on the same level as the similar cornice over the main portal. There is no pediment of any sort over the main portal, which is unusual in Venetian churches. The emphasis on horizontals is very strong, as may be seen in the mouldings that connect the pedestals and the bases of the pilasters atop them in a continuous line, and in the ground-storey entablature which is large and quite pronounced with no decoration at all in its frieze. The façade as a whole is unusual in the way the entire central section of the ground storey projects forward beyond the plane of the flanking sections. While some Venetian church façades have strongly projecting doorways, this is the first in which the whole central section of a façade is treated as a projecting plane.

Plate 42
SAN SALVATORE
Nave, begun 1506. Giorgio Spavento

The plan of San Salvatore, with three San Marco 'cubes' aligned to form a longitudinal church, results in the most complex elevation of any of the Byzantine revival churches. This is particularly apparent in the 'aisles', which consist of an alternation between transverse barrel vaults and lower 'baldachins' with domes on pendentives. In the treatment of the pilasters of the baldachins, San Salvatore shows a systematic development of both Santa Maria Mater Domini (Plates 39, 40) and San Fantino (p.6) for the pilasters that support the nave entablature have rich Corinthian capitals while those that carry the arches around the aisle domes have Ionic capitals. This is the first time that we see full capitals used to distinguish between different support functions and to clarify the organization of a Venetian church.

At San Fantino, the pilasters which carry the aisle arches rise from the floor while those that support the nave entablature rise from pedestals. At San Salvatore, both sets of pilasters rise from the same pedestals, which allows the lower level of the free-standing aisle piers to be the same on all four sides, a more unified treatment than at San Fantino.

The domes of San Salvatore were originally blind, as are the domes of San Marco and all of the other Byzantine revival churches of this period. Lanterns were opened in the domes in the third quarter of the 16th century, and there is now much more light in the church. Later generations seem to have found the Byzantine revival churches too dark for their liking, and almost every one was changed to allow more light.

San Salvatore is the best church built in Venice between San Giovanni Crisostomo and Palladio's San Giorgio Maggiore, begun in 1566. Spavento's imaginative vision allowed him to create an interior that rises from an inventive ground-plan and at the same time establishes strong organizational and spatial values in the elevation. The controlled variety of major and minor spaces is endlessly interesting; the sequence of swelling domes and the rhythm of expanding and contracting 'aisles' gives the nave an almost respiratory quality that is unrivalled in any church in the city.

Plates 43, 44
SAN GIOVANNI ELEMOSINARIO
Exterior and interior, 1527–9. Antonio Scarpagnino

The Jacopo dei Barbari view of 1500 shows on this site the small domed 12th-century church, in some ways similar to the present building, that was destroyed in the Rialto fire of 1514. It is likely that to some extent the new church followed the plan and organization of the old.

The church is set back from the street; shops and houses have been built around and in front of it. There is no façade, only an arch and barrel vault leading to the entrance. While some other churches in Venice are crowded by surrounding buildings, very few are so completely enclosed. That this happened at San Giovanni Elemosinario is probably the result of a desire to use all available space in the Rialto area for shops.

The interior of the church is not very impressive. Despite the quality of the Byzantine revival churches that went before it, San Giovanni Elemosinario is a remarkably plain, awkward, almost ugly building. It has irregular crossing piers that result in pilasters of varying widths; under the dome the longitudinal arches are wider than the transverse ones, as is the case in the four corner chapels as well. The capitals of the crossing piers are stretched across their pilasters with no concern for consistent proportions. These capitals are rudimentary, and seem to have been designed to allow for varying widths with as little difficulty as possible. The minor pilasters which support the side chapel arches have no capitals, only horizontal mouldings, and while this system is somewhat close to Santa Maria Mater Domini, it is much less carefully thought out. As at San Fantino there are groin vaults in the corner chapels rather than domes, perhaps an economizing measure. The east end of the church has been extensively reworked; the low dome with oculus over the choir dates from the late 16th century.

San Giovanni Elemosinario is perfunctory, and while it may be that funds were short and the building carried out in the cheapest possible manner, it is nevertheless the case that the Byzantine revival formulae were repeated here without any conviction or very much thought. Within a very few years the forms of the revival had entirely lost their appeal to the Venetians, who, in the second quarter of the 16th century, preferred church plans based on open squares covered by flat ceilings, as at San Giuliano (Fig. 14).

Plates 45, 46
SAN FELICE
Exterior and nave, begun *c.* 1531

The two-storey main façade of San Felice, with its single portal, a pair of round-headed windows lined up with the aisles, and a central oculus in the upper level, follows the type which Codussi adapted at San Michele in Isola (Plate 4) and San Giovanni Crisostomo (Plate 36). In the articulation of the upper storey the anonymous architect of San Felice shows that he was fully aware of the problems Codussi had tried to deal with in his two earlier façades, but he departed nonetheless from the line Codussi followed. Rather than trying to make the quadrants over the aisles mesh with the pilasters framing the central section of the upper storey, the architect left them very simple: they meet the pilasters without cutting them. This meant that the architect had to give up the idea, to which Codussi appears to have been committed, of giving the quadrants and the semi-circular pediment over the central section the same profile and equal projections from the plane of the façade. Codussi's aspirations have been abandoned in favour of a simpler and more workable, but ultimately less interesting, system.

The main façade portal derives from the main portal of San Giovanni Crisostomo; it has a triangular rather than a segmental pediment, but the same type of capital. The transept portal of San Felice, on the other hand, represents a break from the Codussi tradition, and reveals its 16th-century date in its Ionic capitals.

The interior of San Felice is simple but effective. The barrel-vaulted nave and choir are each two bays long. A crossing is formed by short barrel-vaulted transepts only as wide as the aisles. In the choir the aisle bays at the crossing are open, but those toward the altar are closed to create sacristies. The choir is somewhat unusual in that it ends in a flat wall and not an apse.

The decorative system of San Felice is a combination of the Codussi churches of the 1490s. It resembles Santa Maria Formosa in the absence of capitals on the piers that support the nave entablature, but it is quite close to San Giovanni Crisostomo in the tall pedestals of the piers, the full entablature in the nave and pendentive domes in the aisles. The pedestals, however, are given more elaborate decoration, with inset marble *tondi*, than in the earlier churches.

San Felice rather studiously ignores the developments and

elaborations of Venetian church architecture of the previous thirty-five years. This probably resulted from the conservative taste of a particular parish priest or a wealthy patron. The church is a reconfirmation of the first-generation Byzantine revival style of the late 1490s that had gradually been changed and Romanized in the following three decades: a kind of Byzantine revival revival. It indicates the strong reactionary current that was always a force in Venetian patronage.

Plate 47
SAN GIOBBE
Grimani Chapel, early 16th century; and Martini Chapel,
1471–6

Set into the north flank of San Giobbe is a row of chapels that
vary widely in their size and form (Plate 24). The two closest to
the façade are in some ways similar to each other, but it is the
second chapel which is the more interesting. It is in fact unique
in Venice. It was built for the Martini family, silk merchants
from Lucca, in the early 1470s. In most if not all respects it is
not Venetian but Florentine. In the contrast of the dark stone
trim on the light walls it suggests the Florentine preference for
pietra serena and light stuccoed walls (Fig. 11). The pilasters
are fluted in the Florentine manner, not decorated with vine
tendrils or flowering stalks as the façade portal of San Giobbe
itself (Plate 26), its choir (Plate 25) or Santa Maria dei Miracoli
(Plate 29). The treatment of the inside corners with pilasters
that are creased to lie on two adjacent walls has its origins in
Brunelleschi's Old Sacristy at San Lorenzo and the Pazzi
Chapel in Florence. Venetian architects preferred to leave such
corners undecorated (Plate 29). The chapel is covered by a
pendentive dome decorated with glazed terracotta tiles imported from Florence. This appears to be the earliest use of
this dome type in Venice although it would soon be taken up by
Codussi at San Giovanni Crisostomo. The programme, with
five roundels containing representations of Christ in the centre
and the four evangelists in the corners, is taken from the Chapel
of the Cardinal of Portugal in San Miniato in Florence, built
in the 1460s.

Although the Martini Chapel exerted an influence on the
Grimani Chapel to the west of it, it did not have any discernible
important effect on Venetian architecture. It must have been
regarded as a curiosity and perhaps as interesting and attractive,
but it was too far out of the mainstream of local tradition, and
lacked the necessary authoritative presence, to make an
impression on patrons or architects. Its most uniquely Florentine feature, the glazed pendentive dome, was replaced in
the Grimani Chapel by a dome on pendentives. In one detail
the Martini Chapel did influence some later buildings. The
decoration of the main arch over the chapel entrance, with its
bunches of fruit and leaves, reappears in the arch over the high-
altar chapel of Santa Maria dei Miracoli (Plate 29).

Plate 48
SAN LIO
Gussoni Chapel, *c.* 1490. Pietro Lombardo?

The Gussoni family were prominent residents of the parish of
San Lio; their house (Plate 61) is not far from the church. Their
chapel and the palace are frequently attributed to Pietro and are
both decorated in a similar style. The two works make one of the
only cases in which there is a clear stylistic consistency in the
domestic and religious works carried out for a specific family.

A small, private area of worship, the chapel is framed by
highly decorated pilasters supporting a very lavish entablature
that carries an arch with a bracket keystone. The plan of the
chapel is roughly square, with a shallow niche behind the altar.
Probably to avoid overlap with the altar, carved in smaller scale
but in the same style, the entablature which extends down the
side walls of the chapel was not continued around the marble-
lined niche. In the pendentives are half-length relief figures of
the four evangelists. Above a dentil moulding is a ribbed melon
dome of the sort known from Florentine family chapels of the
first half of the 15th century, such as the Pazzi Chapel in Santa
Croce. While perhaps the family or the architect wanted to
imitate Florentine forms in the chapel, the broken surface of the
dome is at the same time clearly consistent with the rest of the
decoration. Although there was no carved decoration in the
sections of the dome, traces of paint suggest that the urn and
vine pattern of the pilasters was extended over almost every bit
of available surface.

Plate 49
SANTI APOSTOLI
Cornaro Chapel, *c.* 1495. Mauro Codussi?

The Cornaro Chapel is a funerary chapel; there are tombs on each of the side walls. The date of the chapel is established by the fact that we see it clearly in the Jacopo dei Barbari view of Venice of 1500. While this tells us only that the exterior shell of the chapel was complete, one may assume that the interior was at least designed by that time.

The chapel is very unusual for Venice in the last years of the 15th century because of the way the free-standing corner columns, the strongly projecting cornices they carry and the arches of the pendentives are distinct from the wall surfaces. This very rational articulation of an architectural system within a neutral shell suggests that the architect was Codussi for, of all the architects working in Venice in the last years of the 15th century, he was the only one who showed a concern for such clear and coherent systems. The decorative carving of the chapel is restricted almost entirely to the cylindrical pedestals of the corner columns and the fluting on the column shafts. While at the Gussoni Chapel the carving of the entrance pilasters and the entablature above them is so dense that the architectural integrity of each part is sometimes obscured, at the Cornaro Chapel the more limited carving serves to distinguish the elements clearly from one another; the corner columns, already free-standing, are separated more emphatically from the walls behind them by the strong fluting of the shafts. The difference between the Gussoni and Cornaro chapels seems to summarize perfectly the differences between the styles of Pietro Lombardo and Codussi, and represents well what we can establish as the main lines of their thought, even if neither of these buildings can be attributed with absolute certainty to those architects.

Plate 50
SAN GIOVANNI CRISOSTOMO
Bernabò Chapel, 1499–1502

The Bernabò Chapel projects from the north arm of the church. It is wider than it first appears in this photograph, extending laterally on each side of the barrel vault under flat ceilings, as the arm opposite, visible in Plate 38, does not.

The Bernabò Chapel is framed by piers which support an upper level of pilasters and by free-standing columns rising from cylindrical pedestals to carry an arch. There is a great deal of odd cutting and fitting in the chapel. The columns, which were supplied by Pietro Lombardo, were too short when they were delivered, and had to be heightened by the insertion of the pedestals under them. Opposite these columns, on the far wall of the chapel, are pilasters that carry the north end of the barrel vaults. Disproportionately tall pedestals had to be put under these pilasters so that both the pilasters and the columns that jointly carry the barrel vault could be the same height, and rise from the same level.

On the altar of the Bernabò Chapel is a large marble relief of the *Coronation of the Virgin*, carved by Tullio Lombardo between 1500 and 1502. The design of the chapel itself seems to have been used by Tullio as the basis for the architectural setting of the sculpted scene, which shows a barrel-vaulted space framed by pilasters and an entablature and with lateral extensions. The primary focus is on its far wall; above the figures of Christ and the Virgin, God the Father looks down on the scene, as He would look down from a position in the barrel vault of the Bernabò Chapel. This striking resonance between an altarpiece and its setting is unprecedented in Venetian architecture and sculpture.

Plates 51, 52
SAN MICHELE IN ISOLA
Emiliana Chapel. Interior and exterior, 1527–30. Guglielmo
dei Grigi (known as Guglielmo Bergamasco)

All of the other Venetian chapels considered here are structures
whose most important element is their interior. The Martini
and Cornaro chapels have simple exteriors that are given no
decoration at all. The Emiliana Chapel is quite another matter,
and if it is perhaps too much to suggest that the exterior is more
important than the interior, quite clearly more attention was
lavished on it than was the case with any similar chapel structure in the city. This is surely due to its highly visible location
right next to Codussi's façade, which has never in the time since
it was built lost its reputation as a work of major importance.
Some of the most peculiar features of the Emiliana Chapel,
such as its Istrian stone dome (domes in Venice are usually
covered with lead sheets), must be the result of the concern to
treat the chapel in a manner consistent with the white façade
of the church.

The Emiliana Chapel is hexagonal in plan, with deeply
fluted columns which rise from projecting pedestals at the
corners and carry an entablature which breaks forward at an
angle over them. The placement of roundels, ellipses and diamonds of coloured marble in the pilasters, frieze and niche
frames recalls the façade of the Scuola San Rocco (Plate 86)
begun a few years earlier.

The interior of the Emiliana Chapel is extremely bright, lit by
large oval windows in each of its six sides. The decorative
system consists of a pair of fluted columns on tall pedestals in
each corner which carry coffered wall arches over the oval
windows. The high pedestals seen here tend to dwarf the door
frame between them. The six sides of the chapel have alternating doors and altars. One of the doors opens into the chapel from
the church, another from the outside; the third (Plate 52) is
false. The spaces around the doors, and the frieze around the
entire chapel, are filled with a profusion of inlaid stone squares,
circles, rectangles and ovals that seem small and fussy compared to the paired columns.

The treatment of the corners of the Emiliana Chapel may
have been inspired by the Cornaro Chapel (Plate 49), but
Bergamasco chose not to extend the projecting entablature
around the entire interior as was done there. Instead he emphasized the continuation of the vertical lines of the columns
into the wall arches by treating the part of the entablature
between the windows as a low relief.

The critical appraisal of the Emiliana Chapel has varied considerably over the centuries. In 1778, in his study of 16th-
century Venetian architects and sculptors, Tommaso Temanza
praised it enthusiastically, saying that it was 'so judicious and so
decorated' a building that it was justifiably numbered among
the very best in the city. He tells us that as a young man he
measured and drew the chapel with care, and thus had an opportunity to discover the ingenious interrelationships of its
elements. In the late 19th century, however, Pietro Paoletti
wrote that through a careful examination of the chapel 'the first
favourable impression is disturbed, then vanishes to give way to
something that resembles disgust'. He took great exception to
exactly those qualities Temanza praised, saying that 'even a
slightly trained eye will not fail to notice the inelegant proportions of the openings', and criticizing the awkward treatment
of the decoration in the abrupt shifts in scale from the very
small to the heavy and solid.

There can be little doubt that the chapel suffers from the
perpetual and inescapable confrontation with the façade of the
church, for it is not a major architectural work. But neither is it
without real interest and, given the location of the chapel, the
stone dome is quite effective.

Plate 53
PALAZZO BERNARDO
c. 1440

The Palazzo Bernardo has a four-storey elevation and, as was usual in such buildings, it is the third level which was given the most elaborate treatment. The tracery of the central windows on that level, including the lion heads and the rosettes between the arches and *quattrefoils*, is based on the loggia of the Palazzo Ducale, but the tracery of the four windows in the two flanking sections is more elaborate and smaller in scale. The greater height and heavier forms of the central windows of the third storey create a focus there. The dwarf balustrades in the four central windows were common in the 15th century, but there are not many examples of them left in Venetian palaces. The windows on the second level are much simpler, with no tracery, and are the same all the way across the façade.

The Palazzo Bernardo is particularly interesting in that while the windows of the flanking sections are exactly lined up one above the other, the central six-window sections are not. This casual attitude toward vertical alignment in the most important area of the façade indicates clearly that the architect was more concerned to create strong contrasts of pattern and lively decorative effects than to establish a system in which the co-ordination of horizontals and verticals played a major part. The two main storeys of the palace may have belonged to two families or two branches of the same family, but it is nonetheless a curious fact that the main window sections are unaligned. This façade seems almost spontaneous, rather than the result of clear or carefully applied logic.

Plate 54
PALAZZO PISANI-MORETTA
c. 1455

The Palazzo Pisani-Moretta shows interesting variations in the tracery of its two upper storeys. The *piano nobile* tracery is of a fairly common type (see Plate 53), ultimately derived from the Palazzo Ducale; on the axis of each column, between the two parts of the reverse-curve arches it supports, is a roundel with a *quattrefoil*. On the level above, however, the pattern changes: semicircular tracery connecting every other column intersects to form simple pointed arches; roundels with *quattrefoils* matching those of the *piano nobile* rest on the points of these arches rather than between them on the columnar axis, as on the *piano nobile*. This new style of tracery seems to have been de-veloped around 1450, and is known from a few other palaces built at that time.

The Palazzo Pisani-Moretta might be understood as a derivation, somewhat simplified and regularized, of the Cà d'Oro (Fig. 15). The rather spiky effect of the tracery of the Cà d'Oro is substantially softened in the later palace, but the same concern for the creation of richly varied screens is to be seen in the centre.

The difference in the balustrades of the central sections of the two upper storeys is also interesting. On the *piano nobile* there is a shallow balcony; on the top storey the balustrade simply connects the columns. This way of distinguishing be-tween various levels of the building by a number of small and subtle differences is characteristic of Venetian palaces, and this particular arrangement was to reappear in several later works.

Plate 55
PALAZZO MINELLI
Garden loggia and exterior staircase, 1497–9. Giovanni Candi

Plate 56
PALAZZO CONTARINI DEGLI SCRIGNI
Rear view

The spiral staircase of the Palazzo Minelli (also known as the Palazzo Contarini al 'Bovolo', the Venetian dialect word for snail) is one of the most open and airy ever built in Venice. Venetian builders sometimes resorted to spiral staircases which projected from the body of a building in order to save precious floor space, but the few such arrangements of this sort still to be seen in the city have their steps enclosed in a cylindrical shaft, like the one at the Palazzo Contarini degli Scrigni (Plate 56), and are really interior staircases with small windows for light. It is not only in palaces that such staircases are to be found, for in the church of Santa Maria dei Miracoli (Plate 28) a spiral staircase projects from the body of the church building in the angle between the choir and nave.

The design of the Palazzo Minelli staircase results from the extension of a garden façade of five arcaded storeys to different levels of this projecting spiral staircase. As the storeys of the garden arcade are not of equal height, and the builder found it necessary to do a great deal of cutting and fitting, the turns of the staircase from one level to another are not always evenly spaced. This is most apparent in the way the ends of the stone steps, which are visible in the brickwork, at times rest directly on the arches of the level beneath them, and at other times are separated from them by several courses of brick. The change in the shapes of the arches, and the constant shift of columnar proportions from one level to the next, might have disturbed an architect or patron who demanded Classical orthodoxy and consistency, but in the late 15th century Venetians did not yet make these demands. What mattered most was the open, lacy effect and not proportional commensurability of one part to another.

The emphatic contrast of the small arches of the staircase and the larger ones of the loggias, and the vertical division of the whole façade into two sections of different scale and pattern, were probably not regarded as a great disadvantage. The way in which this was turned to good effect reveals the lingering Venetian delight in open columnar screens and Gothic asymmetries. From several points of view, despite its very late 15th-century date and Classical vocabulary, this façade is basically Gothic in spirit, and recalls the rich, perforated and textured façades of the late 14th and early 15th centuries, such as the Cà d'Oro (Fig. 15).

In most respects the Palazzo Minelli garden loggia and staircase were quite without influence in Venice, but there is perhaps a trace of the effect of the design in the elevation of the courtyard of the Fondaco dei Tedeschi (Plate 101), begun only a few years later.

Plate 57

CA DEL DUCA

Basement and south-west corner. Begun 1457; work
suspended 1461. Bartolomeo Buon

The Cà del Duca (House of the Duke) was begun for the Venetian Andrea Corner in 1457. It was sold in 1461, in a still very
incomplete state, to Duke Francesco Sforza of Milan. With the
change of ownership there was much correspondence between
the Duke and his representatives in Venice about altering the
design of the palace, and there was some strain with the architect, who refused to show his model of the building to the
Duke's representatives. A description of the state of the building
when it was offered for sale corresponds quite closely to what
we see today as the only part of the 15th-century design that was
finished, and it is generally assumed that not much work, if
any, was actually done on the building under the Duke's
architects.

Had the building been completed it would have been the
largest private palace in Venice at the time, and one of the
biggest ever built. Its foundations were later employed to
carry two separate palaces, each quite substantial in size. Even
in its truncated state the Cà del Duca is powerful and impressive, and introduces several new features to Venice. The variety
of the sharply accented stonework of the basement and ground
floor is in marked contrast to any building built in the city
before this time. The basement level in most Venetian palaces
is usually completely undecorated; here it is composed of carefully marked Istrian stone blocks. In this detail the Cà del Duca
influenced a number of later palaces (Plates 63, 65). The faceted
blocks of the ground storey are also a novel element in Venice.
The slightly projecting corner units of the palace derive from a
fortified castle tradition quite foreign to Venice. The only
other building in our period that shows such a feature is the
Fondaco dei Tedeschi (Plate 100). The un-Venetian massive-
ness of the ground storey is indicated by the size of the portal
on the side canal. The large full columns set into the edges of
the corner units are so thick that in order for them to be well
proportioned the ground floor of the palace would have to be at
least twice as high as it is now.

A few years after he began the Cà del Duca, Buon enlarged
the Arco Foscari (Plate 71), and in that work, on a much reduced
scale, we find an idea first considered at the Cà del Duca: the
columns set in corners.

Because of its unprecedented size and decoration, the Cà del
Duca had no important effect on Venetian palace architecture
for well over a century and a half. In the late 16th century a new
element of gigantism began to appear in Venetian palaces, and
in the 17th century the unfinished building exerted some influence; the ground-floor stonework pattern of Longhena's
façade of Cà Pesaro (begun in 1673) resembles that of the Cà del
Duca.

Plate 58
PALAZZO MOROLIN
c. 1485

Of the Venetian palaces of the late 15th century one of the most original is the small Palazzo Morolin, which has been called an example of 'almost sublime incoherence'. Bilaterally symmetrical, the palace has a central section slightly higher than the two which flank it. On the *piano nobile* of this section is a unit with four round-headed arches supported by thick columns. This is strongly marked at bottom and top by the balustrade and a projecting cornice respectively. In each of the flanks, on the same level as the windows in the central section, is a pair of widely spaced pointed-arch windows with roundels on either side of their finials. On the upper level of the canal façade are smaller windows, in plain frames, which maintain the spacing of the *piano nobile*; those in the centre are rectangular, those in the two wings slightly lower and with round tops.

In the palaces of this period we have seen combinations of late Gothic and Classical elements, but no façades in which the two styles are distributed in different parts of the façade to create a system based on their contrast. While there are several palaces in which a central section is marked out by decorative elements and understood to be separate from the flanking sections, there are no others in which the distinction is accomplished through the juxtaposition of contrasting styles and an uneven roof line.

The date of the palace is uncertain, the architect unknown. On the basis of the exquisite piercing of the balustrade on the side of the palace it has been suggested that the architect was a Lombard, but attributions of buildings based on single details are not generally useful; the stonecutter who carved the balustrade may have nothing at all to do with the design of the façade.

Plate 59
PALAZZO ZORZI A SAN SEVERO
c. 1480. Mauro Codussi

Recent investigations have revealed that the Palazzo Zorzi was built in several stages. Around 1480 a series of older, irregular and oddly aligned buildings was covered with a new canal façade. The concern to organize uneven buildings behind a regular façade is characteristic of the later 15th century, not only in Venice, but in many other parts of Italy.

There is no documentary evidence for the attribution of the Palazzo Zorzi to Codussi; its main support is the rationality of the façade and the fact that Codussi had known the owner, Marco Zorzi, at San Michele in Isola, where he was one of the most important patrons of the Camaldolese monastery.

The long canal façade is divided symmetrically into three sections: two wings with three rectangular *piano nobile* windows flank a central section with nine round-headed windows. The projecting lintels over the windows in the flanking sections become the top impost block cornices of the central windows in an interesting way. Over the lintels of the rectangular windows are roundels which rise to the same moulding as the arches over the windows of the central section, creating a unique pattern.

The balusters of the small balconies in the two outer sections of the façade suggest that these are later than the long balcony in front of the central windows. That balcony breaks forward slightly in front of the middle window only. Originally the elements of the façade must have been arranged to project increasingly from the edges to the centre, an unusual arrangement in Venetian palaces of this period, when central balconies generally projected uniformly.

Plate 60
PALAZZO ZORZI A SAN SEVERO
c. 1480. Detail of façade. Mauro Codussi

One of the most interesting apsects of the façade design of the Palazzo Zorzi is the way in which the architect tried to align the window frames of the mezzanine with the elements of the *piano nobile* above it. In the *piano nobile* windows there are both fully round columns and half-columns; on the mezzanine the short fluted pilasters framing the small rectangular windows vary in width according to whether they are on the axis of a full or a half-column. The determination to make these pilasters correspond to the forms above them sometimes has curious results: when one of the double *piano nobile* windows is framed by a free-standing column on one side and a half-column on the other, the mezzanine window beneath it is framed by pilasters of sharply unequal width.

The combination of extreme rationality and *naïveté* which produced such an arrangement seems to have been charac-teristic of Codussi until about 1485. Apparently his first palace, the Palazzo Zorzi reveals the same interest in carefully consistent systems that is observed on the façade of San Zaccaria. In his later palaces, as in his later church façades, Codussi abandoned his quest for total consistency in every detail in favour of larger overall clarity.

Plate 61
PALAZZO GUSSONI
1480–90. Pietro Lombardo

The Palazzo Gussoni is one of the relatively few surviving small houses with extensive sculptural embellishment. The house was originally even smaller than it is now. The top floor is very different in style and decoration from the two below it. The strongly projecting brackets above the *piano nobile* are of a form that occurs only in a terminating cornice, never between storeys, which indicates that the palace was heightened by the addition of the top storey, as was the house to its left.

The entire façade of the Palazzo Gussoni is revetted with Istrian stone rather than stucco-covered brick, the usual treatment for small houses, as may be seen in the houses on either side of it, and in Plate 62.

Every window and door frame on the Palazzo Gussoni has been decorated with Lombard-style carving of vines, vases and rosettes. Under the *piano nobile* windows is a row of pilasters that is rather unusual – a purely decorative extension of the window rhythms. Above the *piano nobile* windows are urns with carved flames, and above the narrow alley to the left of the palace three tiers of projecting brackets make the shape under the *piano nobile* at this point interesting and unexpected. The architect did not try to make the façade symmetrical, probably because of the lack of space.

Perhaps the Gussoni family was unable to afford or did not want a larger house on a wider canal, but clearly they did want their house distinguished from those of their neighbours.

Plate 62
HOUSE IN CAMPO SAN SILVESTRO

This small, utterly plain house represents one end of the spectrum of decorative possibilities in Venetian domestic architecture. While there are a great many lavish palace façades that represent the other extreme (see Fig. 15), and books on Venetian architecture tend to give the impression that every building in the city is a major monument, there is as well a vast matrix of largely or totally undecorated houses such as this that are in a real sense 'styleless'. It is as simple as it can possibly be; the wall is plain stuccoed brick and the Istrian stone window frames have not a single feature that is more than the bare structural minimum. As a result it is extremely difficult to date; it could be as early as the 14th century, or as late as the 18th.

This undecorated house offers an interesting contrast to the Palazzo Gussoni (Plate 61) which is in fact not much bigger, if at all, but which boasts stone revetment and richly carved window frames, pilasters, mouldings, cornices and water-gate. Thus, to a shell such as that of the Campo San Silvestro house, the 'style' and the 'architecture' would have been added in the form of carved decoration of door and window frames, mouldings or cornices between the storeys and across the top of the façade, or frames in the fields between the windows, according to the owner's taste and budget. It is probably not an overstatement to suggest that for the late 15th century the difference between the Palazzo Gussoni and the house in Campo San Silvestro would have been seen as the difference between 'architecture' and mere 'construction'. It is a modernist bias to see no distinction between structure and architecture; in the 15th and 16th centuries such a view would have been incomprehensible to the majority of people who thought about the buildings around them. The 'architecture' would have consisted more in the carved decoration of the building than in any of its structural elements, or in any abstract proportions of wall, window or interior space.

Plate 63
PALAZZO CORNER-SPINELLI
c. 1485–90. Mauro Codussi

In terms of its departure from Gothic traditions and the presentation of new possibilities, the Palazzo Corner-Spinelli is analogous to the façade of San Michele in Isola or the church of Santa Maria Formosa. Although the Palazzo Corner is not documented, for many years it has been attributed to Codussi. The similarity of the ground-floor stonework to the lower part of San Michele in Isola, and the traceried windows, in which the central form is not a perfect circle but an inverted tear drop, identical to those in the clerestory of San Zaccaria, support the attribution. More important than the details, however, it is the thoughtfulness and intelligence of the façade that most suggest Codussi.

For the first time an architect has applied a number of Classical elements to a Venetian palace; the pilasters at the edges of the façade and the garland-and-roundel frieze of the upper storey are unprecedented. It is in the tightness of its organization, however, that the façade constitutes a quantum leap. On the upper levels all the horizontals are continued across the façade and tied to the pilasters. The tops of the window balustrades are linked to the upper part of the pilaster pedestals by mouldings that continue across the areas of wall between them. The uppermost element of the *piano nobile* entablature becomes the decorated edge of the projecting balconies of the top storey.

The taller ground floor did not allow Codussi to keep the pilasters of all the storeys uniform, and on their pedestals those of the two upper levels are rather squat. If the design is not without its inconsistencies of Classical proportion, it still shows a greater cohesiveness than any façade built in Venice up to that time.

Not all of the elements of the façade are Classical, and one is particularly unexpected. The lobed balconies of the *piano nobile* are rare in Venice, and these seem to be based on a late Gothic example in Verona. They are part of the original façade, and indicate that, despite his new ideas, the architect's mind was not yet closed to Gothic forms, and that his fancy could still be caught by an unusual and attractive detail which he then copied in his own work.

Plate 64
PALAZZO VENDRAMIN-CALERGI
c. 1500–*c.* 1508. Mauro Codussi

The most Classical palace built in our period, the Palazzo Vendramin is a profound development of Codussi's earlier, more uncertain design of the Palazzo Corner-Spinelli (Plate 63). Built originally for the Loredan family (its present name identifies its subsequent owners), it is sometimes known as the Palazzo Non Nobis from the Latin inscription, now difficult to see, across the ground storey. The opening words of Psalm CXV: 'Not to us O Lord, not to us, but to thy name be the glory given', seems an attempt to anticipate and defuse charges of excessive sumptuousness by suggesting that the palace was built to the glory of God and the city and not of the Loredan family.

Although orders extend across the entire façade, and for the first time we find identical window treatment on all storeys (an idea which never became popular in Venice), the palace front is much less uniform than it is made to seem, for it is in fact superbly manipulated to achieve the effect of even storeys. On the ground floor the pilasters and windows rise from the same level; every vertical element has a moulded base. On the *piano nobile* fluted wall columns rise from pedestals which are as high as the balcony balustrades; unfluted window columns and half columns rise directly from the balcony floors. On the upper storey there are no balustrades; unfluted wall columns rise from bases which rest on the *piano nobile* entablature. The bases of the window frames and central columns are eliminated here. As a result the windows of the upper level appear cut off by the *piano nobile* entablature as those on the *piano nobile* are cut off by the balustrade. In this way the upper storey was lowered without appearing to shorten the windows.

The illusion of perfect continuity created with this system was well appreciated by later architects working in Venice; Michele Sanmichele used it in exactly the same way at the Palazzo Grimani a San Luca (Fig. 16), where the *piano nobile* pedestals, hidden by balustrades, were eliminated, along with the balustrade itself, on the upper storey.

Although the architectural system of the Palazzo Vendramin-Calergi façade is strongly Classical, there is still an obvious concern for rich and colourful effects; the marble revetment is white and yellow, and subtle touches of blue-gray marble, porphyry and *verde antico* make this one of the most sumptuous palaces façades in Venice, as well as the most rational.

In the richness of its design and the brilliant handling of its details, the façade of the Palazzo Vendramin-Calergi is as effective as any to be found in Italy in this period, and one of the finest ever built in Venice. No palace in Florence or Rome of these years shows a more thoughtful assimilation of Classical ideas and a more sensitive reconciliation of antique forms and local architectural tradition.

Plate 65

PALAZZO MANZONI-ANGARAN

c. 1485–90

The façade of the Palazzo Manzoni-Angaran is revetted with Istrian stone and marble. The tradition of different window designs on each storey is modified: the windows are the same on all three levels but the colour of the stone is different in each. In earlier palace façades, such as the Palazzo dell'Ambasciatore (Plate 13), framed fields around the flanking windows were stuccoed while the rest of the façade was exposed brick. At the Palazzo Manzoni-Angaran a similar contrast is achieved on the upper storey by setting the flanking windows in a panel of Istrian stone and revetting the wall with marble.

The fluted pilasters that divide the two upper storeys show a new concern for correct Classical forms, but there is at the same time an awkward and un-Classical juxtaposition on the ground storey between the tall, slender pilasters that frame the water-gate and the stubbier ones to either side which divide the centre from the flanking sections.

One very curious feature of the façade is the way the outer frames of the outermost windows of the central *piano nobile* section do not match the columns that separate the central windows, but match instead the window frames of the flanking sections, despite the fact that these two sets of windows are separated by a large pilaster.

The quincunx pattern of the roundels between the flanking windows of the *piano nobile* is also seen at the Cà Dario, which appears to date from the same years. The rich garland and putto frieze on the entablature over the ground storey is fuller than that of the Palazzo Corner-Spinelli (Plate 63) which seems to have inspired it.

The Palazzo Manzoni-Angaran, in its reduction of the rich variety of Venetian façades to a more even and coherent system, belongs to the same class of transitional buildings as the Palazzo Corner-Spinelli, and if it is a bit less striking in its originality, it is nonetheless an important work.

Plate 66 (*overleaf*)

SCUOLA GRANDE DI SAN MARCO

Façade. Begun *c.* 1488 by Pietro Lombardo and Giovanni Buora; completed *c.* 1495 by Mauro Codussi

The façade of the Scuola San Marco is often taken as representative of architecture in Venice, its colourful effects being paralleled to the paintings of Giovanni Bellini as something fundamentally Venetian. While it is not representative of architecture in Venice in the whole of the later 15th century, in its richly coloured and encrusted decoration it does represent the style of the 1480s. This decade saw the creation of some of the most decorated works of the second half of the century, among them Santa Maria dei Miracoli (Plate 12), Codussi's façade of San Zaccaria (Plate 8), the Scala dei Giganti (Plate 79), the east courtyard façade of the Palazzo Ducale (Plate 91) and the Cà Dario (Plate 16).

On the basis of the Scuola San Marco façade, characterized by asymmetry, a non-Classical organization of proportions, extensive decoration and, in the placement of the narrative reliefs flanking the portals, a lack of interest in consistent perspective organization, Venetian architecture has been seen as the polar opposite of Florentine. If the rich and colourful effect of the façade is sometimes regarded as a positive virtue, the rejection of ideas dear to the Florentines, and therefore to many who measure architecture by a Tuscan rule, has led some people to conclude that in the late 15th century Venetians were still too limited by their past to understand new ideas.

As always it is dangerous to generalize about Venice. The bright colourism of this façade may have been intended to make it resemble the basilica of San Marco, thus linking buildings with identical dedications by means of their architectural character. It has been suggested that the lobes of the façade, particularly the three on the left, are intended to recall the domes of San Marco.

The façade of the Scuola is at a right angle to the façade of Ss. Giovanni e Paolo, and some of the forms, such as the free-standing columns of the main portal of the Scuola and the heavily projecting lunette above, may have been designed to be seen with the portal of the church (Plate 2).

The absence of Classical severity and exact symmetry do not indicate a lack of comprehension; the façade is perfectly appropriate for the building behind it, which **is** strongly asymmetrical in its interior forms and function.

Plate 67
SCUOLA GRANDE DI SAN GIOVANNI EVANGELISTA
Staircase, 1498. Mauro Codussi

The visitor to the Scuola San Giovanni passes through the doorway seen in Plate 83, turns to the left, and sees one ramp of the staircase rising in two flights to the upper storey of the building. In this work Codussi's experience and experiments with changes of axis at Santa Maria Formosa, with a series of domes in the ambulatory of San Zaccaria, and with the first of his double-ramp staircases at the Scuola San Marco, are brought together in one of the finest spatial and decorative sequences in all Venetian architecture.

At two points in the climb to the upper storey the visitor must change direction 90 degrees: on the ground-level landing and on the upper one. At these points are domes on pendentives. Above the mid-flight landing, where no change of direction is possible, the horizontal barrel vault continues the only line of access. The entablature under the barrel vault is supported at the lower and upper landings by full pilasters which rise from pedestals, but at the mid-flight landing only consoles carry the horizontal stretch of the entablature, which de-emphasizes the separateness of the landing.

The staircase decoration is very carefully arranged to augment the spatial effects, and is much richer on the upper landing. The only free-standing columns are found there, and the arches across the barrel vault are wider and more extensively decorated at that point as well. A large window floods the upper landing with light. Codussi placed flat elements in the darker areas and fuller ones where there is the most light to model them. From the bottom the carefully wrought total effect is of a staircase that rises and expands into brighter light and swells with more plastic architectural forms. Few staircases anywhere so subtly and effectively convey the greater importance of their upper level, and so fully clarify the lines of access to it.

Plate 68
PALAZZO CONTARINI DELLE FIGURE
1504–46. Antonio Scarpagnino?

The Palazzo Contarini gets its nickname 'delle Figure' from two figures under the *piano nobile* balcony (invisible in this photograph). The palace is sometimes attributed to Scarpagnino on the basis of its similarity to some of his work (Plate 91). There is documentary evidence that work on the site began in 1504, but the style of the façade suggests that it was not designed until about 1520.

The wide and fairly open design of the façade is one of the more interesting of this period. Entirely revetted in Istrian stone, it is unusual for the pediments over the *piano nobile* windows. The architect wished to preserve the traditional arrangement of a pair of windows to each side of a central group of connected windows. He accomplished this by the surprising use of pediments over each of the flanking windows, and a wider, higher one over all four windows of the central section. It seems that the precedent of arched windows on the *piano nobile* was too strong to allow the use of rectangular windows, despite the fact that they would have been more consistent with the straight entablatures that crown them.

The upper storey is too low to allow for pediments. At this level the contrast of the window pilasters with the four wider pilasters that mark off the three sections of the façade is awkward, but it is the unavoidable result of the desire to frame the upper windows like the ones beneath them.

Plate 69
PALAZZO GRIMANI A SAN POLO
c. 1500–*c.* 1520

The date of the Palazzo Grimani is uncertain; while it does not appear in the Jacopo dei Barbari view of 1500, it might have been designed as early as the first years of the 16th century. The identity of the architect is also unknown; it has been connected to both Codussi and to Buora. The attribution to Codussi seems unlikely, for the de-emphasis of the relief is quite different from his latest works, the upper staircase landing of the Scuola San Giovanni Evangelista (Plates 84, 85) and the Palazzo Vendramin-Calergi (Plate 64).

The almost equal height of the three storeys and the equal width of the flanking and central sections make this one of the most regular façades of the period. The carved decoration between the windows of the flanking sections is not unusual (Plate 64), but its extension to all three storeys appears here for one of the first times. The idea was taken over at the Palazzo Contarini delle Figure.

The pediments over the ground-floor windows seem to be additions, for they are inconsistent with the rest of the façade. The use of roundels to fill the spaces above the columns of the two upper storeys and between the windows, shows a concern to balance the large, dark openings of the windows with flat and colourful accents. The concern is not for the development of thick sculptural elements but for flat patterns within a tightly organized grid.

Plate 70
ARSENALE PORTAL
1460. Antonio Gambello

The Arsenale portal carries the date 1460 on the pedestals. The inscription on the frieze and some commemorative sculpture were added in the 16th century. Originally there was a small drawbridge leading to the gate; the fixed bridge and small enclosure in front of it are 17th-century additions.

The Venetians' view of themselves as 'new Romans' received its clearest architectural expression at the Arsenale. As the heart of the city's naval life, both military and mercantile, the Arsenale was a place of fundamental importance for Venetians, and to emphasize the idea of Roman inheritance the entrance to the maritime centre was through a Roman gate. It is interesting that the capitals of the ground-level columns are not Classical, but 12th-century Byzantine pieces in re-use. The architecture thus fuses the two sources of Venetian culture into a single work.

At the Arsenale the paired columns on pedestals, and the entablature that breaks forward over them, are derived from the Arch of the Sergii in Pula (Fig. 1), but while at Pula the piers of the central arch rise from pedestals as high as those supporting the columns, at the Arsenale they rise directly from ground level, as they do in triumphal arches in Rome and Verona.

For the upper part of the Arsenale portal the architect had no Roman model to draw on, and this level is not Classical. Its contrast with the lower storey is interesting, and the overall design may be subtler than it first appears. The idea may have been to imitate those cases in which Roman architecture was re-used. Perhaps we are meant to suspend disbelief so far as to imagine that the Arsenale was built around a Roman arch to which a top storey was added in a different, later style. Venetian historical myths would have been well served by such a notion.

Plate 71
PALAZZO DUCALE
Arco Foscari, 1450–85

The Arco was begun in the reign of Doge Francesco Foscari (1423–57) and still bears his name, although it was considerably elaborated by later Doges. It was built in two distinct stages between 1450 and 1464, and then given its sculptural embellishment of pinnacle figures in the 1480s.

An important recent study has determined that the lower central section, consisting primarily of the red and white striped arch around the opening of the Porticato Foscari, is the original portion of the structure, dating from around 1450. In the second stage of construction, carried out between 1462 and 1464 under Doge Cristoforo Moro, framing piers with columns set into their corners were added to the original arch and the entire structure was carried up another storey. This phase of the work is reasonably attributed to Bartolomeo Buon, on the basis of stylistic similarities in the portal of Ss. Giovanni e Paolo (Plate 2) and the Cà del Duca (Plate 57).

The Arco reveals the tendency in Venetian civic architecture to establish richly decorated focal points along major visual and ceremonial axes. The Arco functions very effectively in two different views. From the east it frames the entrance to the Porticato Foscari. From the south, seen against San Marco, it serves almost as a transept façade of the church, and many of its important architectural elements, such as the double order of columns on the ground level, the balustrade, the columns on the upper level, the pinnacles and the figure sculpture which crowns them, are derived from the Gothic west façade of the basilica.

The Arco Foscari is characteristic of Venetian architecture in the later 15th century in that it contains both new elements and long-established ones. Columns of Classical proportion and architectural forms with a new sense of weight are combined with Gothic foliate decoration, elongated pyramidal roofs, and a concern for effects of rich colour and texture that are a major part of the Venetian tradition.

Plates 72, 73
SCUOLA GRANDE DI SAN MARCO
Ground-floor hall, *c.* 1487–90. Upper hall, *c.* 1490–5; ceiling *c.* 1515; high altar 1533–46

On the left side of the ground floor of the Scuola is a large hall with two rows of columns down the centre. These support the major meeting room of the confraternity (Plate 73) directly above. The columns lead back from the façade entrance to a large doorway at the opposite end, which once led to a water-gate on a rear canal since bridged over. They continue the line of free-standing columns on pedestals flanking the main entrance (Plate 66) – for the first time in this period an attempt is made to relate the exterior and interior elements of a building. It is difficult, however, to establish whether the colonnades were planned before or after the façade was designed, or at the same time. The contract for laying their foundations dates from January 1488, before Pietro Lombardo and Buora were on the project.

The sculptural decoration of the ground-floor hall is limited to the door frames of the two staircase ramps and the rear entrance, and to the square pedestals and capitals of the central colonnades. The pedestals are carved with leaf, vine and urn patterns which are quite close in style to the decoration of the church of Santa Maria dei Miracoli (Plate 12) and the atrium of the Scuola San Giovanni Evangelista (Plate 81). Such decoration is often associated in particular with Pietro, who is documented at the Scuola San Marco from mid-1489 to the end of 1490.

Despite its relatively simple treatment, the hall was to have a major influence thirty years later on the ground-floor hall of the Scuola San Rocco (Plate 86).

In the 1490s, the upper hall of the Scuola San Marco was perhaps the largest room in Venice outside the Palazzo Ducale, and by the 1560s, when its decoration was complete, one of the richest.

Membership in the *scuole grandi* was open to the nobility, but the positions of honour and authority were reserved for the middle class. This arrangement was viewed as providing a healthy outlet for the administrative aspirations of the middle class, who were in their turn excluded from participation in the government of the Republic. It is not surprising that the *scuole* came to regard themselves as miniature governments, and that their main meeting halls came to resemble those of the

Palazzo Ducale. The similarity in this case extends beyond the size and shape of the hall to its extensive pictorial decoration, now dispersed, by Tintoretto, its richly carved gilt coffered ceiling and the elevated area at one of the narrow ends.

Originally the architectural decoration of the upper hall was restricted to the door frame around the staircase landing and to the ceiling. The windows in the west wall are very simple, and on the interior even lack carved frames. In the 1530s a large altar was designed for the north end. The fluted Corinthian columns by Sansovino are totally different from the late 15th- or early 16th-century work at the Scuola.

Plate 74
PIAZZA SAN MARCO
Clock Tower. Central section 1496–9; wings 1502–6; upper wing storey and terrace 1755–7

Until the late 1490s the 12th-century Procuratie Vecchie extended east past the spot where the Clock Tower now stands, as we see in a painting by Gentile Bellini (Plate 94).

In 1493 a new clock was commissioned by the city, but not until 1496 was the decision made to place it over the entrance to the Mercerie, the main street that runs from San Marco to Rialto, and funds appropriated for a suitable building. This was what is now the four-storey central bay of the tower. It was originally within the fabric of the Procuratie, with three bays of the older building extending to the east of it, as we see in the Jacopo dei Barbari view (Plate 95). Between 1502 and 1506 wings were added. In the mid-1750s eight columns were added to the ground storey, two in each of the wing bays, and the top storey of the wings, set back to form a terrace, was built.

It is not clear if the original design of the Clock Tower included the wings. The two-stage construction is not regarded by all scholars as proof of a two-part design process. While it is possible that a full design was built in phases because of financial restrictions, it is also quite possible that the tower was at first intended to be an elaboration of only the bay of the Procuratie around the entrance to the Mercerie.

The decoration of the Clock Tower is restricted to the centre bay, where the rich face of the clock and the walls of the storeys above create a variety of patterns. The wings were deliberately played down so as not to detract from the original part of the structure. The cornice over the central arch, for example, has small brackets on it, but these were not carried to the wings. The pilasters of the wings, although as tall as those of the central section, are slimmer, and from straight on give the illusionistic impression of being set back, an effect to which the smallness and simplicity of the windows also contribute.

The combination of antique-derived forms and the very decorative treatment of the clock face and upper storeys is characteristic of the Venetian attempt to fuse the patterned exteriors of the Palazzo Ducale and San Marco with a system of Classical orders; to preserve the traditional and embrace the antique revival.

Plate 75
PIAZZA SAN MARCO
Campanile. Begun *c.* 912; upper section completed 1513;
entire tower rebuilt 1902–12

The bell tower was begun around 912 but probably not finished
until the late 12th century. Struck by lightning several times,
the upper part, originally built of wood, required frequent
repairs. When it was struck yet again and badly damaged in
1489, the decision was made to rebuild the top in stone and
brick. That year Giorgio Spavento was paid for a design, but
nothing was done on the project for more than twenty years.
During the delay a temporary wood and tile top was built to
protect the shaft. This provisional covering appears in the
Jacopo de Barbari view (Plate 95). After an earthquake further
damaged the tower in 1511, the rebuilding of the upper section
was finally begun, under the supervision of Bartolomeo Bono,
proto of the Procurators of San Marco. The work was carried
out quickly; on 6 July 1513 the gilt bronze angel was hoisted
to the top with great celebration.

   The upper part of the tower consists of an open arcaded belfry, a closed brick section above it and a tall pyramidal roof.
This disposition of elements follows that of the old tower. The
design is severe and straightforward; even John Ruskin, who
detested most Venetian architecture of this period, could not
object to it much, and even praised the way the scallop shells
terminate the large flutes in the tower shaft. The mouldings and
cornice project strongly to compensate for the strongly foreshortened view from the Piazza below.

   On 14 July 1902 the original bell tower collapsed on itself in a
neat heap, miraculously sparing San Marco and the Palazzo
Ducale and only slightly damaging one corner of the Library,
although the Loggetta at its base was completely crushed. The
city government resolved that day to rebuild the tower 'where
it was, as it was'. The reconstruction was completed in 1912.

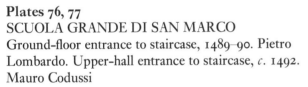

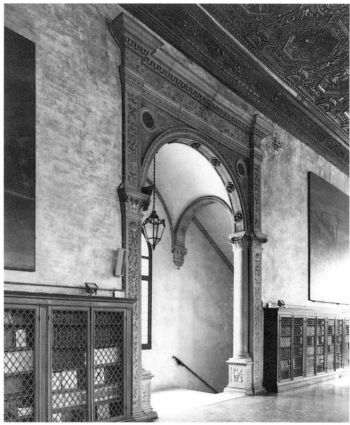

Plates 76, 77
SCUOLA GRANDE DI SAN MARCO
Ground-floor entrance to staircase, 1489–90. Pietro
Lombardo. Upper-hall entrance to staircase, c. 1492.
Mauro Codussi

The late 15th-century staircase at the Scuola San Marco was torn down in the 19th century. In the early 20th century it was reconstructed, badly, from what original stones could still be found. In its present form the staircase is crude and awkward, and gives a misleading impression of the original.

At the bottom of the ramps are landings roughly square in plan with pendentive domes; the upper landing, much less square, also has a pendentive dome. Over the stairs is a flat ceiling and, as is clear in Plate 77, the transitions are clumsy. Not all of this is due to the 20th-century reconstruction, for the difficult and cramped site made the original awkward.

When Codussi replaced Pietro as *proto* in 1490, most of the work on the ground floor was probably complete, but not much on the upper, and the staircase was not yet done. In style the door frames on the ground floor are different from the upper one, and seem to be a little earlier. The most obvious dif-ferences are the placement of the columns of the *piano nobile* door frame on carved pedestals, and the elimination from this frame of the segmental pediment. On the *piano nobile* the door frame, with its horizontal top, rises almost to the level of the ceiling, and seems to help support it. The looser relationship between the ground-storey doorway and ceiling is thus avoided. An argument in favour of the attribution of the *piano nobile* door frame to Codussi is the fact that in its elimination of the segmental pediment and its extension nearly to the ceiling it is very close to the arrangement of the ground floor at the stair-case entrances of the Scuola San Giovanni Evangelista (Plates 83, 84) which is documented to Codussi.

Another interesting difference between the two doorways at the Scuola San Marco is the treatment of the columns them-selves. On the ground floor they are half-columns attached to piers; on the upper level the pier is hollowed out behind the columns and the shaft seems to stand free in a channelled frame. It is possible that there were different designers for the two levels, but the carving on the pilasters and friezes of the two doorways is quite similar in style and execution, which suggests that the same crew of stonecutters worked for two consecutive chief builders with different ideas.

Plate 78
SAN GIORGIO MAGGIORE
Façade of dormitory wing, begun 1508. Giovanni Buora

On the lagoon end of an extremely long dormitory corridor, this façade indicates clearly the lingering fondness for skylines with curved shapes. The three semicircular tympana do not correspond to any roof line behind them; they are there purely from an aesthetic preference. In the early 16th century there must have been a number of such façades and the Venetian enthusiasm for them may have arisen from a desire to refer to San Marco whose grouped domes such shapes resemble.

Buora had worked at the Scuola San Marco (Plate 66) in the 1480s, and it is sometimes argued on the basis of the similarity between the skyline of the façade there, particularly the right wing, and the dormitory façade of San Giorgio Maggiore, that it was he who was responsible for the upper sections of the Scuola San Marco. The suggestion is interesting but not conclusive, for Buora could have copied a form on which he had worked earlier but did not design.

The tight grid of the façade with every window arch and oculus frame tangent to a cornice is similar, although obviously in much reduced form, to the treatment to be observed in palace façade design in the second decade of the 16th century (Plates 68, 69).

Plate 79
PALAZZO DUCALE
Scala dei Giganti, begun *c.* 1485. Antonio Rizzo

Plate 80
THE PRESENTATION OF THE VIRGIN Jacopo Bellini
1460–70. London, British Museum

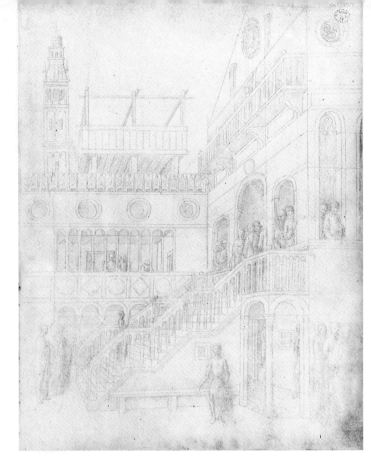

Called the Scala dei Giganti after Jacopo Sansovino's large figures of Mars and Neptune on the upper landing, the staircase dates from soon after the fire of 1483. On the basis of the Jacopo Bellini drawing, it can be concluded that in rebuilding the staircase Rizzo based his design heavily on a pre-existing one rather than creating a totally new form.

The three arches on the upper landing are the only round ones on the *piano nobile* (Plate 90) and their arrangement, with a slightly higher central arch, recalls Roman triumphal arches. A small prison cell under the steps housed traitors and special enemies of the state so that the Doge would ceremonially tread on them as he went up and down the stairs.

The staircase is a focal point at the north end of the courtyard, and much attention was given to its flank elevation. The decorative elements were worked together into a tightly interlocking system. The top of the bench and the third step form a continuous horizontal; above the bench the wall is divided into panels by pilasters which form continuous verticals with the balustrade piers.

The small scale of the flank decoration is in marked contrast both to the courtyard façades and the piers supporting the lateral projections of the upper landing; rather than try to fuse the flanks and the façade, Rizzo emphasized the differences between them by dramatically shifting the scale of their decorated forms. The contrast is deliberately drawn, for example, between the lintel over the window and the pier capital next to it; and between the light balustrade grill work and the heavy roundel above the arch right alongside it.

The Jacopo Bellini drawing is an important document of Venetian architecture from several points of view. The central element of the scene is a staircase which is extremely close in design and scale to the Scala dei Giganti. The bench along the flank of the staircase with the window above it, the projecting wings formed by round arches at right angles to each other, the three round arches off the wide landing at the top of the stairs,

and the placement of the staircase in a corner formed by buildings of unequal height, are the same in both the drawing and the Scala dei Giganti.

The Scala dei Giganti was not built until after Bellini's death, so the drawing must be based on an older staircase, one which stood on the same spot as the Scala dei Giganti. The ceremonial elements of the old one were carefully preserved in its rebuilding.

The primary difference between the two staircases is the number of steps. In the drawing there are fifteen, in three flights of five. This is iconographically significant: the Presentation of the Virgin took place in the Temple of Solomon on a staircase which had, according to long tradition, fifteen steps.

The use of the main staircase in the courtyard of the Palazzo Ducale to represent a major ceremonial access to the Temple implies the identification of the palace with the Temple of Solomon. The tremendous importance of justice and wise rule in the Venetian self-image made an association of the Doge and Solomon almost inevitable, and recognizable elements from the Palazzo Ducale came to be used in the late 15th and 16th centuries to evoke Solomonic settings, as may be seen not only in drawings by Jacopo Bellini, but in paintings by Titian and Bonifazio Veronese as well.

Plate 81
SCUOLA SAN GIOVANNI EVANGELISTA
Atrium, completed 1481. Pietro Lombardo

The enlargement and reorganization of the Scuola San Giovanni Evangelista in the late 15th century began with the creation of an elegant public vestibule and a private inner courtyard. The atrium consists of architectural decoration applied to the exterior walls of the two flanking buildings, and an entrance wall between them across the inner side of the area; the outer side is open along a street. The atrium portal, which would have been closed with wooden doors or wrought-iron gates, was the only entrance to the inner courtyard.

Rising from a base decorated with rosettes, fluted pilasters with characteristically Lombard capitals carry a richly carved entablature which breaks forward over each capital and over the entire width of the door in the end wall. Above the pilasters on the side walls are urns with carved flames, very similar, but not identical, to those found on top of the three tympana on the right-hand side of the façade of the Scuola San Marco (Plate 66). Between the pilasters of the side walls brick is covered with stucco painted to look like veined marble panels set in a dark border. On the end wall the revetment is real marble and the decoration is in general much richer. The concentration of the decoration on the end wall, and the use of stucco instead of marble revetment on the side walls, is similar to the original treatment of the interior of Santa Maria dei Miracoli (Plate 29), where Pietro began to work as the *proto* in 1481, just after the completion of this atrium.

The two windows and the door frame in the central wall are extensively carved. In the semicircular tympanum over the doorway is a large carved eagle, the symbol of St John the Evangelist, with the gospel in his talons. At the outer edge of the entrance wall two kneeling angels adore the Cross atop the tympanum; the Scuola's prize possession was a relic of the Holy Cross.

There is no exterior civic or ecclesiastical architecture in Venice that is all like the atrium of the Scuola San Giovanni Evangelista. The notion of creating a rich entrance wall on one space leading to another closed and private space behind it may have come from contemporary ideas for monastic choirs; the closest analogy to the atrium is the Frari choir-screen (Plate 20), on which Pietro appears to have worked. As decorative elements that serve to enrich the approach to a reserved area of the institution, the two works are variations on one idea. It is interesting, and characteristic of the *scuole*, that the inner courtyard is not decorated in any impressive way. Except for the doorway into the ground floor of the Scuola San Giovanni Evangelista (Plate 82), not built until about thirty years later, the private zone of the courtyard is quite unimpressive. There was obviously a greater concern to create a rich public area than to reserve all the decoration for the *scuola* membership.

Plate 82
SCUOLA GRANDE DI SAN GIOVANNI EVANGELISTA
Ground-floor portal, lower level dated 1512

Two large doorways lead into the ground-floor rooms from the inner courtyard of the Scuola. One, just visible at the right-hand side of this photograph, is rather plain, and dates from the early 15th century if not before. Another, much more decorated one, carries the date 1512 in the frieze under the pediment.

The earlier door is opposite the staircase entrance seen in Plate 83. The 1512 door opens into another part of the ground floor, and is not aligned with any interior element, but it is roughly on the axis of the atrium portal (Plate 81). It is difficult to determine where the main entrance to the Scuola was in the late 15th century. The 1512 portal might have been an entirely new one built to line up with the atrium, or it might have been the redecoration of a doorway already there.

Although it is clear that the portal was built after the death of Codussi in 1504, it is sometimes suggested that his ideas were the basis for the new design. This is unlikely, for the two levels of free-standing columns and the low triangular pediment over a round arch, unknown in the work of Codussi, belong to a later generation, and are more consistent with the date 1512.

The upper level has a large window derived from the *piano nobile* landing of the staircase (Plates 84, 85) surrounded by pilasters and a frieze decorated with roundels and diamonds. It is not on the axis of the portal below it, and was probably neither designed nor built at the same time, dating instead from the time when the tracery pattern of the upper staircase landing was extended to the windows of the *piano nobile* hall of the Scuola.

Plate 83
SCUOLA GRANDE DI SAN GIOVANNI EVANGELISTA
Ground-floor entrance to staircase, 1498. Mauro Codussi

The ground floor of the Scuola San Giovanni Evangelista is fairly low. Rather than attempt to disguise this limitation, Codussi turned it to good effect by raising the door frame around the staircase entrance all the way to the ceiling beams and emphasizing the horizontal of the entablature by enlarging the egg-and-dart moulding of the cornice and decorating the frieze with an inlaid pattern of palmettes on a black background. The horizontal orientation of the frieze palmettes is a curious feature; in most Classical and contemporary Venetian examples palmettes – decorative forms derived from palm fronds – are aligned vertically (Plate 26) as they appear in nature. At the Scuola San Giovanni the pattern serves to emphasize the horizontality of the frieze.

Beyond the doorway is one of the two ground-floor landings of the double-ramp staircase. These landings are covered by domes on pendentives which rise well above the ceiling level of the ground-floor room and are not visible in this view. The contrast between the horizontal entablature of the doorway and the domed space behind it is striking and effective, but at the same time Codussi linked the elements of the doorway with the wall decoration of the area behind it. The pedestal mouldings and panels continue into the landing, and the pilaster edges in the corner of the landing maintain the pilaster and jamb pattern of the doorway. The use of the decoration to establish a connection between the ground-floor portal and the staircase itself was a new departure for Codussi; from what remains of the original staircase at the Scuola San Marco, it appears that there he was limited by a system which was much less coherent and unified. Part of the new unity was achieved through light; at the Scuola San Giovanni Codussi was able to place two windows in each ground-floor landing so that these areas are not the dark spaces they sometimes appear to be at the Scuola San Marco (Plate 76), but are as bright on the inside as the portal that leads to them.

Plates 84, 85
SCUOLA GRANDE DI SAN GIOVANNI EVANGELISTA

Upper landing of staircase from below and from main hall, 1498. Mauro Codussi

On the *piano nobile* landing Codussi brought a wide variety of decorative elements and several different levels of relief into an extremely fine balance. On the outside wall of the landing a large traceried window opens the entire area under the pendentives. This window is quite close in design to the façade windows of the Palazzo Vendramin-Calergi (Plate 64), which dates from only a few years later. The way this window is set under its arch is very thoughtful. On the three open sides of the landing the arches have three rows of coffers and rosettes; on the window side there are only two, but the underside of the two smaller tracery arches is given identical decoration, so that we understand the window as part of the arch next to it rather than something separate.

One of the brilliant touches on the upper landing is the way in which Codussi arranges the free-standing columns in the window wall to serve effectively in two different views. From the staircase the paired columns of the door frame on the inner wall and the two columns next to the window in the outer wall seem to balance, and the two window columns seem to be in roughly the same plane. In the view from inside the upper hall, on the other hand, the architect wanted to have a symmetrical and uniform arrangement of planes from the near doorway to the far window, and here the columns supporting the window tracery do not appear to be paired with the columns that support the inner corners of the landing arches, but to be set between and behind them. The framing of the window columns, when viewed through the doorway opposite, creates a stunning effect of receding verticals and narrowing openings that is quite different from the appearance of the window columns in the view from the staircase.

In the decoration of the base of the upper-landing dome Codussi also showed a keen awareness of the way in which the top of the staircase would be seen from inside the main hall; the base of the dome appears as a curve framed by the opposite curve of the arch of the doorway to the landing. The application of decoration to this element makes the dome base similar to the frieze above the doorway arch, and results in interplay of richly textured curves in three planes.

Plate 86

SCUOLA GRANDE DI SAN ROCCO

Façade, 1517–*c*. 1540. Bartolomeo Bono and Antonio
Scarpagnino

The façade of the Scuola San Rocco presents complex problems
of dating and attribution. The building was begun in 1517 by
Bono, who was replaced by Sante Lombardo in 1524. In 1527
Scarpagnino became architect of the project, which was complete by the late 1540s. There is insufficient documentation to
determine how much of the façade Bono had designed or built
before he was fired in 1524, allegedly for not having made much
progress on the job, but probably because of disagreement over
several aspects of the Scuola design.

Several elements of the two storeys are stylistically at odds
with each other. The ground-storey bays, with double windows
derived from Codussi and broad frames around them inlaid
with squares and circles of coloured stones, are quite flat. In
sharp contrast, the upper storey has pairs of round-headed
windows framed by full columns on tall cylindrical bases and
topped by pediments. The powerful relief of the upper floor,
seen also in the boldly projecting brackets that carry the
columns, which may derive from the *piano nobile* of the Cortiletto dei Senatori in the Palazzo Ducale (Plate 92), indicates a
different personality from the one that created the ground-level
window bays. It seems likely that Bono designed the lower bays
and Scarpagnino the upper.

The large free-standing columns and broken entablatures of
both levels are closer in spirit to the style of the upper storey,
which suggests that Scarpagnino added them when he designed
the upper level.

The lighter relief of both storeys of the right-hand bays
preserves the pattern of the Scuola San Marco (Plate 66) where,
as here, the secondary entrance is smaller and the decoration of
the right-hand side in general less extensive.

Plate 87

SCUOLA GRANDE DI SAN ROCCO
Ground-floor hall, begun 1517. Bartolomeo Bono and
Antonio Scarpagnino

In many ways the ground-floor hall of the Scuola San Rocco is
a recapitulation, in up-to-date style, of architectural ideas
from the Scuola San Marco and the Scuola San Giovanni
Evangelista. The major element of the room, the double colonnade carrying an open beam ceiling, is copied from the Scuola
San Marco (Plate 72), although its vocabulary is very different.
The windows in the hall are derived from the upper landing
window of the Scuola San Giovanni Evangelista (Plate 85).

The style of the architectural elements of the Scuola San
Rocco is much heavier and more Classical than that of the
Scuola San Marco. Here the tall pedestals of the colonnade are
octagonal, with inlaid marble panels. The general thickening
of the forms is observed in the ground-floor windows also. At
the Scuola San Marco the windows on both storeys are relatively small, single lights with no tracery; here they have
become double openings with heavy tracery. The difference
between the Scuola San Marco and the Scuola San Rocco is
parallel to that observed between the churches of the 1490s,
such as San Giovanni Crisostomo (Plate 38), and the heavier,
more Classical interiors of a decade later, such as San Salvatore
(Plate 42).

Plate 88
SCUOLA GRANDE DI SAN ROCCO
Ground-floor hall. Staircase entrance portals, begun 1545.
Antonio Scarpagnino

The design of the staircase at the Scuola San Rocco was the source of considerable disagreement among the architects, the officers of the Scuola and even the city government. Several plans were considered and rejected, including one by Bono, the *proto* of the Scuola from 1517 to 1524. Friction over the staircase design probably contributed to Bono's dismissal. Despite Bono's insistence that the staircase design chosen was wrong for its setting, it was finally completed by Scarpagnino in the early 1530s. It soon became clear that Bono had been right, and the directors of the Scuola decided in 1545 to tear down the ill-conceived staircase and start all over again on a new design by Scarpagnino. The Council of Ten, the branch of the Venetian government that supervised the affairs of the *scuole*, out of patience with the indecision, ordered the directors of the Scuola San Rocco to model their new staircase on the examples of the Scuola San Marco and the Scuola San Giovanni Evangelista. Imitation had become an official policy.

While the earlier double-ramp *scuola* staircases are parallel to their ground-floor halls, with the ramps meeting at a landing on the upper floor, the staircase ramps at the Scuola San Rocco are at right angles to the main hall. Two lower ramps rise to a landing from which a single upper ramp turns back 180 degrees and continues to the main hall above (Plate 89). Scarpagnino seems to have been concerned to follow the dictates of the Council of Ten, but at the same time to create a new form.

Plate 89
SCUOLA GRANDE DI SAN ROCCO
Upper ramp of staircase, 1545. Antonio Scarpagnino

A clear effect of the order that the Scuola San Rocco build its staircase on the pattern of those of the Scuola San Marco and the Scuola San Giovanni Evangelista is seen in the upper ramp. At the top of the staircase at the Scuola San Giovanni Evangelista there is a landing with a dome over it just off the main hall (Plate 85). At the Scuola San Rocco, despite the fact that in many ways his staircase design departed from his models, Scarpagnino placed a dome over the upper end of the staircase, off the main hall. But there is no clear, separate space below it: there is no landing at the top of the ramp; the stairs rise directly to the edge of the upper-hall floor. The curious result is a dome on pendentives over steps and not a landing.

With the stairs approaching the upper hall at a right angle, the architect had the choice of making the view from the hall reveal a descending barrel vault or a continuous horizontal one extending to the exterior wall of the Scuola. He chose the latter, increasing the contrast between the shallow lower ramps and the much deeper top one, and the spaces seem to lack coherence.

The Scuola San Rocco staircase is not the equal of the one at the Scuola San Giovanni Evangelista. Where Codussi maintained perfect control over every aspect of the design, from the large spatial sequence to the subtlest scaling of the architectural elements within that sequence, Scarpagnino seems to be struggling to keep everything together, and not always successfully.

Plate 90

PALAZZO DUCALE

Courtyard. East Façade, begun *c.* 1484, completed *c.* 1550.
Antonio Rizzo (to 1497), Pietro Lombardo (1497–*c.* 1510),
and others

After the east wing of the palace, containing the Ducal apartments and several major state reception rooms, was seriously damaged by fire in 1483, Rizzo was commissioned to rebuild it. He began at the north end of the east wing, in the area around the Scala dei Giganti (Plate 79), which he also rebuilt. In the course of the 16th century the rebuilding gradually proceeded south, maintaining the late 15th-century design; the entire wing was completed around 1550.

In 1497 it was discovered that Rizzo had embezzled a large sum of money from the palace workshop treasury. Rather than face charges he fled the city, and was replaced by Pietro, who seems to have enjoyed a reputation as a diligent, efficient and honest man. He probably made only slight changes, if any, to Rizzo's design; most attempts to find the seam between the work of one master and another have not been completely convincing.

Rizzo gave to the palace courtyard a new appearance, building the east façade in Istrian stone, richly decorating it in Classical vocabulary with garlands, ribbons, arms and armour, and roundels with marble and porphyry inlays. Although the decorative motifs are, with the exception of the pointed arches on the *piano nobile*, all classically derived, the façade is consistent with the Venetian Gothic tradition, represented by the Cà d'Oro (Fig. 15), of extensive surface elaboration in which regular rhythms are willingly sacrificed to richness of effect.

The east wing, particularly the two upper storeys, makes a curious impression on the viewer who expects to find the uniformity that would have characterized such a project in Florence or Rome at the end of the 15th century, but in fact the design is perfectly suited to its function and location and is quite satisfying. On the ground floor and the *piano nobile* the façade is opened by long arcades in an arrangement that was taken over from the exterior of the Palace (Plate 93). There was nothing in the loggias at these levels that interrupted the even placement of the arches except for the Scala dei Giganti close to the north end. The upper levels of the façade, on the other hand, had to cover a series of irregularly sized and arranged rooms. The exterior window placement was determined by interior spaces which could only be slightly reorganized; so a decorative system was developed for the façade which did not depend on even rhythms and could accommodate extreme irregularity without appearing distorted. Seen from the palace courtyard the east wing appears as a richly brocaded surface on which almost no wall area is left unpierced or unsculpted. The spaces between the windows are treated as framed fields of sculptural decoration, and vary from single to double and from narrow to broad panels.

One entirely misunderstands Venetian architecture of the late 15th century if one concludes that this façade is the result of architects merely compromising a regular design in order to accommodate interior spaces. There is great delight here in the syncopated rhythms of the arch and window openings, the occasional alignment of the windows of the two upper storeys and the careful creation of varied textures. The façade should be regarded, as it surely was in the 16th century, as a highly successful and aesthetically satisfying work. If it is different from the more uniform and subdued forms we expect in Florence and Rome, it is not in any way inferior. The façade is, like the city itself, varied, irregular, richly textured, and never boring or predictable. It offers a perfectly viable aesthetic alternative to Classical uniformity, and in such works as this, can be regarded as better and more successful.

Plate 91
PALAZZO DUCALE
Courtyard. North façade, *c.* 1520. Antonio Scarpagnino

In the north-east corner of the courtyard of the Palazzo Ducale is a small area almost entirely closed off by the Scala dei Giganti and the Arco Foscari. This space is called the Cortiletto dei Senatori (Little Courtyard of the Senators) because it appears that the members of the Senate gathered here during state ceremonies. The Cortiletto is bounded on the north by a two-storey façade. Both the ground-level arcade and the upper entablature of this façade are continued from the east wing with no significant changes, but on the *piano nobile* a new style appears, different from any other part of the palace courtyard. On this level the most interesting aspect of the treatment is the very strong relief of the forms, especially the window frames. In order to support the cylindrical bases, which project too far from the wall simply to be hung on it, the architect placed a row of consoles with small Ionic volutes. A similar idea had appeared earlier in Venice, on the canal flank of Santa Maria dei Miracoli (Plate 12), where the consoles that support the pilasters are much shallower. The closest parallel in the architecture of the 1520s is found on the *piano nobile* of the façade at the Scuola San Rocco (Plate 86), which is also connected with Scarpagnino.

The *piano nobile* of the north courtyard façade is close in style to the *piano nobile* of the Palazzo Contarini delle Figure (Plate 68) and is therefore datable to the period around 1520, a date supported by the fact that in 1523 Titian painted frescoes (now lost) in a room behind the north-wing windows.

The relief of the *piano nobile*, with its strongly projecting columns and pediments, is in clear contrast to the late 15th-century style of the two upper storeys of the east wing of the palace (Plate 92), where the articulation of the surfaces is not as sharp, deep or uniform, and where the wall is conceived very differently. On the east wing the elements seem carved out of the wall, while on the north wing the fuller window frames seem applied to the wall. Perhaps because the *piano nobile* of the north courtyard was on the same level as the pointed arch arcade of the east wing (see Plate 90), the design of the window frames was made heavier here than those on the east so as not to be overwhelmed by the strong relief of the piers and arches next to them. It is characteristic of the architecture of the courtyard in general that the forms selected for the north façade were roughly equal in mass to those of the east arcade, but different in style. This strong contrast between the two wings, and the abrupt change from the pointed arches of the east wing to the triangular pediments of the north wing, were actively sought and regarded positively. In his design for the *piano nobile* of the north wing Scarpagnino appears to have been concerned not to 'harmonize' the new wing with earlier parts of the palace, but to enrich the courtyard by the introduction of new forms. In some respects the deliberate contrast created actually has a precedent: the small scale of the decoration of the Scala dei Giganti (Plate 79) was in equally deliberate contrast to the east courtyard façade from which it extends. The unity of the courtyard is not found in a single style, but in a consistent preference for contrasts of decorative forms. On the east wing there are semicircular arches, pointed arches, and round-headed windows both with and without segmental pediments. But there are no triangular pediments, so these were introduced in the north wing to create an even wider variety of shapes. At the same time this addition makes it clear that the north wing is both part of the courtyard as a whole and partly separate from it; the selection of forms thus clarifies the architectural organization of the spaces of the courtyard.

Plate 92
PALAZZO DUCALE
East Wing. Façade on the Rio della Canonica, begun *c*. 1484, completed *c*. 1510. Antonio Rizzo (to 1497); Pietro Lombardo (1497–*c*. 1510)

The exterior of the east wing of the Palazzo Ducale is dramatically different in style from the south and west wings, just as the east façade of the courtyard is different from the rest. As on the courtyard, the fenestration is very irregular; the vertical alignments are often not maintained through two, let alone three storeys, and the surfaces are extensively pierced. Above the round-headed windows of the first full storey is a frieze decorated with roundels that only rarely line up with anything above them or below. In some places, as in the upper storey, a cornice, obeying its own rules, will break forward over windows, and in other, apparently analogous places, it will not. The wall areas between the windows are not carved on the exterior as they are on the courtyard, but a similar decorative impulse is felt in the strongly patterned diamond-faceted stones of the lowest level of the *rio* façade. Stonework of this kind is unusual in Venice; this is the only example found in our period. While a similar system is found twenty-five years earlier on the unfinished Cà del Duca, there it was used on the ground floor. At the Palazzo Ducale it appears only on the basement level. Differences in the actual stone pattern of the two examples suggest that the Cà del Duca was not the source for this element on the Palazzo Ducale; diamond stonework is well known in cities of the mainland, and appears here to be an import.

On parts of the canal façade, patterns ultimately derived from Classical forms become almost completely abstract. Above the windows of the lowest level are segmental pediments, but they are connected to the vertical frames above them in such a way that the pierced fields over the pediments seem the major forms, and the pediments themselves merely the result of the peculiar shape above them.

The free variations on Classical elements and the decorative system of carefully framed wall panels with almost no two the same size, indicate how far the Venetians could be from an orthodox classicism which requires the even repetition of identical forms. Ruskin, who hated almost all Classical architecture, regarded the *rio* façade 'as an example of finished masonry in a vast building, one of the finest things, not only in Venice, but in the world'.

Plate 93 (*previous page*)
PIAZZETTA SAN MARCO
View from the water

There are very few urban spaces anywhere in the world to compete with the Piazzetta San Marco, and none enjoys so spectacular a location on a broad lagoon. The effect of the view from the water is often described as scenographic, and by this is meant the very carefully arranged contrasts of colour and texture, the lively combination of horizontal and vertical elements and the superbly focused sight-line straight down the central axis of the Piazzetta. In the view from the water the Piazzetta is one of the greatest city stage-sets ever conceived, a perfect theatre for Venetian civic ceremonies.

With the construction of the Library (Plate 99), the Piazzetta was complete, and the view of the Clock Tower from the water was then channelled between the two long and rich but very different façades of the Palazzo Ducale and the Library. One of the happy effects of the addition of the Loggetta to the east side of the Campanile (Plates 75, 98) is to centre the Clock Tower even more precisely by closing off the view of it on the left side as the narthex of San Marco does on the right. As we see the Clock Tower now it is perfectly framed between the two columns that stand at the south end of the Piazzetta, the Palazzo Ducale and the Library, and the Loggetta and the narthex of San Marco. In the Piazzetta the Venetian genius for organizing dazzling combinations of sizes, shapes, textures and colours may be seen its very best. The elements in the view are not tediously symmetrical, but are nonetheless exquisitely balanced; nothing matches, but everything is so exactly placed and so successfully accommodates everything else, that the unity of the whole is guaranteed. It is no accident that the most effective viewpoint is from the water; visitors approaching the city by boat would have been impressed and perhaps intimidated by the splendour of the sight even before they disembarked.

Plate 94 (*above right*)
PROCESSION IN PIAZZA SAN MARCO
Gentile Bellini, *c.* 1496. Detail. Venice, Accademia

For the study of the Piazza San Marco around 1500 we are fortunate to have two views which date from the 1490s: Gentile Bellini's large painting of the procession in the Piazza on the feast of Corpus Domini, and Jacopo dei Barbari's remarkable bird's-eye view of Venice (Plate 95). In the Bellini painting we see the Piazza as it was in the mid-1490s; the detail reproduced here shows the 12th-century Procuratie Vecchie and preserves the appearance of the north side of the Piazza before the construction of the Clock Tower. The entrance to the Mercerie was under the fourth arch from the east end, which was marked as a major passage-way by being slightly higher than the others. The area to the east of the Procuratie, a small piazza now known as the Piazzetta dei Leoncini from two sculpted lions placed there, was changed beyond recognition in the 17th, 18th and 19th centuries, and the visitor to Venice will find nothing there now that resembles the buildings that appear in the painting.

The Bellini painting is quite detailed in many respects, and we can see that the two-storey building had stilted Byzantine arches and short pilasters rising between the *piano nobile* arches to a cornice above, a system known from other 12th-century buildings in Venice.

In this picture of the Procuratie decked with oriental carpets hanging from every *piano nobile* window and crowded with spectators who look out on the activities in the square below, we see more clearly than from any other contemporary source the Venetian love for rich textures and colours, for ceremony and spectacle, and for human movement in a lively architectural setting. The marchers and the spectators become an integral part of the architecture, and the buildings become inextricably bound up with the vitality and life of the people.

Plate 95 (*below right*)
VIEW OF VENICE Jacopo dei Barbari
1500. Detail

The Jacopo dei Barbari view is very helpful for a general idea of the appearance of the Piazza before it was radically transformed by the construction of the wings of the Clock Tower, the new Procuratie Vecchie, the 16th-century church of San Geminiano, the belfry and Loggetta of the Campanile of San Marco, and the Library. In some details, however, such as its indication of the relative sizes of the old Procuratie Vecchie and the Clock Tower, the view is oddly inaccurate. The tower appears to be huge in proportion to the arcade, and the street-level arch over the entrance to the Mercerie is shown as high as the two storeys of the Procuratie. This must be a mistake; even the 12th-century two-storey Procuratie is unlikely ever to have been as low as the central arch of the Clock Tower (Plate 74). Jacopo dei Barbari was often astonishingly precise, and it is difficult to understand this disproportion. In fact, the tower arch is too high, rather than the Procuratie too low, for an extra level appears between the ground-storey columns of the Clock Tower and the arch they carry. The artist must have been working on the view, which was published in 1500, in the last years of the 15th century, just when the Clock Tower was under construction, and he might only have been able to guess at its size in relationship to the arcade of the Procuratie. While unlikely, it is not impossible that the tower as it appears in this view reflects an earlier design abandoned in favour of the present one.

Jacopo dei Barbari's distortion of the Clock Tower may be a measure of its revolutionary transformation of the Piazza area; its importance as the focus of the view from the lagoon (Plate 93) was so new and dramatic that the artist seems to have expressed this inadvertently by showing the Clock Tower larger than it was.

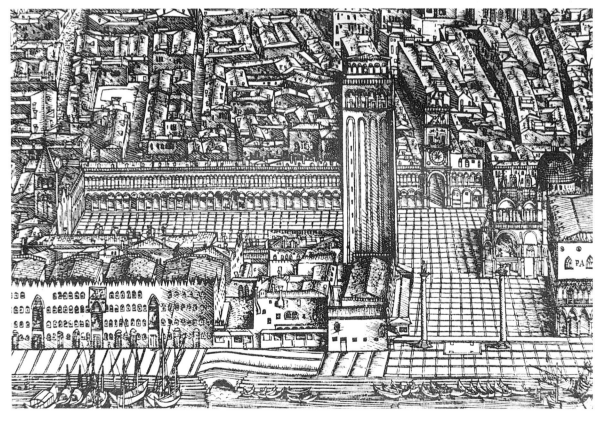

Plates 96, 97
PIAZZA SAN MARCO
Procuratie Vecchie, begun 1514

The rebuilding of the Procuratie Vecchie reveals clearly the strong conservative tendency in Venetian civic architecture in the early 16th century.

In the 1170s, when the Piazza was enlarged to its present size, a two-storey arcade was built along the north side, with a row of shops on the ground level and the apartments of the Procurators of San Marco above (Plates 94, 95). The important and powerful office of Procurator, second in magistrative authority to the Doge, carried with it the right to live in state housing on the Piazza. The number of Procurators gradually increased to nine, eight of whom had quarters in the Procuratie by the 15th century.

By the early 16th century the building was old and getting expensive to maintain in good condition; when a fire severely damaged part of it in 1512, the decision was made to replace it. In its general design the new building is very similar, the major change being the increase in height to three storeys. While the details of the new building belong in style to the 16th century, the whole conception of the Procuratie is 12th-century Venetian in character, and it is better understood as the reconstruction and decorative updating of an old and important building than as a new 16th-century architectural idea.

It fell to Bartolomeo Bono, as the *proto* of the Procurators of San Marco, to construct the new building, but he did not design it. The initial design came from one Giovanni Celestro, an architect whose career is very shadowy.

A careful look at the Procuratie Vecchie reveals an important aspect of Venetian architectural history. While the Procuratie was rebuilt closely along the lines of the previous structure on the site, there is no trace of archaizing in the details. The earlier building had double arches above single ground-level arches (Plate 94) but, beyond maintaining this original non-Classical rhythm, little effort seems to have been made to preserve the decorative elements of the older structure. The square piers on the ground level have bases (part of their pedestals have disappeared through repavings of the Piazza), mouldings and capitals that are not at all Byzantine, and in the two upper levels, with their fluted columns with strongly moulded bases and composite capitals, this is even more the case. Instead of the stilted Byzantine arches of the earlier building we find half-round arches of a much more Classical style. The entablatures of the three storeys are also Classical in profile and proportion, particularly the upper one, which has a bracket cornice. The frieze of the upper entablature is pierced by oculi and creates, with the uneven merlons above, a fringe of alternating lights and darks, wall surfaces and openings, and high and low forms that is characteristically Venetian. However, while the forms are not 12th-century, the mood of the original building is preserved, for we know that the upper part of the earlier Procuratie had a strong and lively alternation of surfaces, shapes, lights and darks.

In the Procuratie Vecchie the traditional Venetian fondness for screens of columns, for the almost textile-like effect of pierced forms creating a rich backdrop for human activity, is seen at its clearest.

Plate 98
PIAZZA SAN MARCO
Loggetta, 1537–*c*. 1545. Jacopo Sansovino. (*See also Plate 75.*)

At the time Sansovino began to transform the Piazzetta with the addition of the Library, there was, at the base of the Campanile, a rather unprepossessing lean-to used as an informal gathering-place by noblemen on state business. The roof of this old structure is just visible in the Jacopo dei Barbari view (Plate 95). As part of the remodelling of the area, Sansovino replaced this old loggia with a new one.

The Loggetta has been called Sansovino's least architectural work because it is in large part the support for a sculptural programme. The architectural members are more sculptural than in Sansovino's other buildings; the columns framing the arches are fully free-standing under projecting entablatures. This arrangement is well known from triumphal arches in Rome, and the three arches of the ground level of the Loggetta and the attic above indicate that Sansovino had in mind such prototypes as the Arch of Constantine.

The sculptural programme is appropriately triumphal in tone. In the ground-level shell niches are Sansovino's bronze figures of Minerva, Apollo, Mercury and Peace. In the central attic panel is Venice as Justice, and in the large panels to the right and left are personifications of the city's two major island conquests, Cyprus and Crete. The four smaller panels show putti playing with Classical armour.

The Loggetta is at one end of a clear axis of richly sculpted architectural accents. At the other end is the Scala dei Giganti (Plate 79), which has a similar triumphal-arch motif in the three arches of its upper landing. It was a stroke of genius to balance the Scala dei Giganti with another, but more classically correct, triumphal arch. It is clear that Sansovino understood past Venetian architecture, and saw its future.

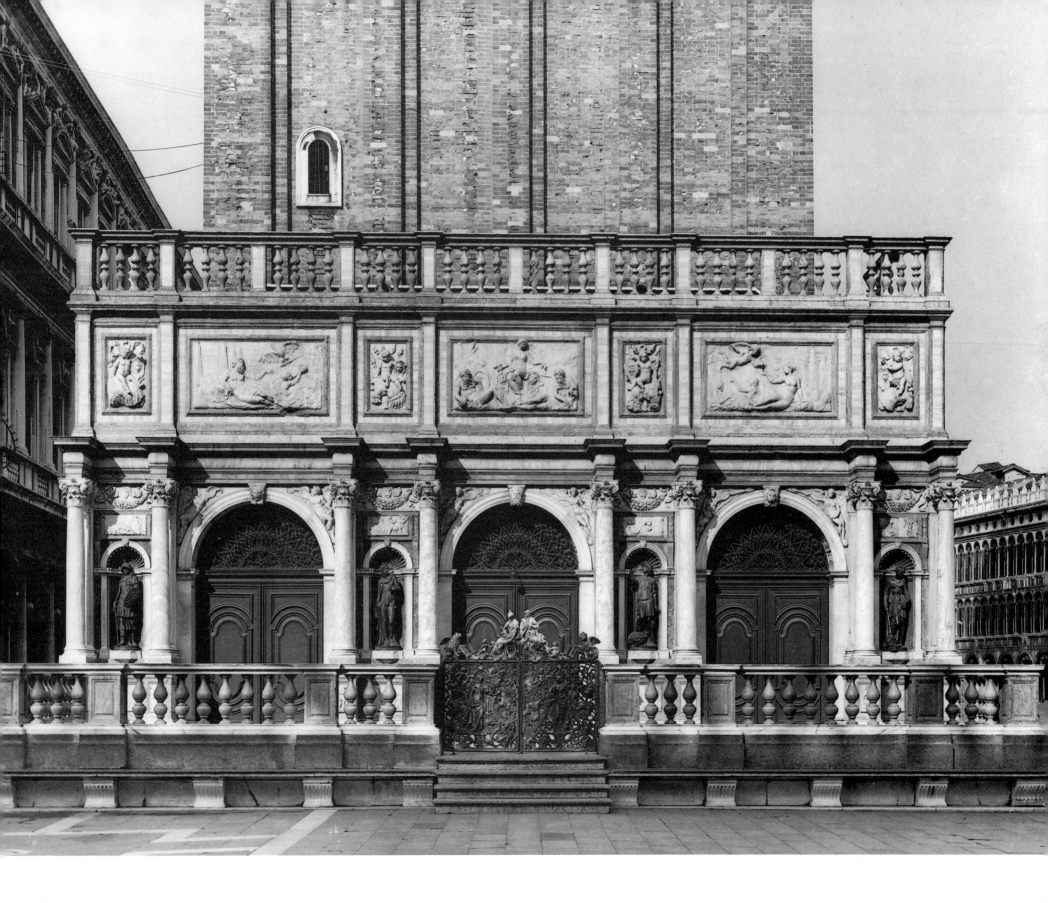

Plate 99
PIAZZETTA SAN MARCO
Library, begun 1537. Jacopo Sansovino

The Library of San Marco represents a major change of direction in Venetian architecture. The monumental quality of the building, the thickness and solidity of its Classical forms, and its grand and stately rhythms, have no connection at all with local civic architectural traditions. Many of the elements of the building, such as the treatment of the corners as the combination of a pilaster and an engaged column, or the fenestrated and garlanded frieze with putti placed over the columns to emphasize the structural system of the façade, have been traced to specific buildings in Rome and Tuscany under construction and known by Sansovino before he left Rome for good in 1527. The classically orthodox sequence of Roman Doric on the ground storey and Ionic on the *piano nobile* was also new in Venice, and the sculptural decoration of the whole, with reclining river gods in the spandrels of the ground storey and winged female figures on the level above, is richer than anything that had been produced even in Rome up to that time.

In the placement of the figure sculpture in the spandrels there is an interesting recollection of Classical ideas about the orders: Doric was regarded as solid, strong and masculine, while the Ionic was held to be more elegant, graceful and feminine. That there are male figures in the ground level and female above is surely not coincidental, and indicates a more consistently learned approach to architecture than is to be observed in Venetian buildings before this time.

In only two ways do local traditions seem to have determined the appearance of the Library: in the choice of Istrian stone as the material for the façade, and in the idea of a very long arcade on a public space, which had been a Venetian preference since the Procuratie Vecchie had been built along the Piazza in the late 12th century. It is a remarkable fact that the Library, although it does not correspond to the Palazzo Ducale stylistically, goes with it very well to form the Piazzetta. The powerful density of the Library, little more than half the height of the Palazzo Ducale, effectively balances the taller and airier palace, and it is a measure of Sansovino's skill that he could introduce a new Classical style to Venice in the same building with which he completed the Piazzetta in a manner consistent with Venetian ideals.

With the Library Sansovino established himself as the most up-to-date and important architect in Venice, and secured for the Roman Classical style a firm place in Venetian architecture. From the late 1530s there was no turning back to the styles of the previous decades.

Plate 100
FONDACO DEI TEDESCHI
Courtyard

The courtyard of the Fondaco dei Tedeschi was originally open to the weather. The present skylight, a 20th-century addition, gives the modern visitor the very misleading impression that it was intended to be understood as an interior.

As with the outside of the building, there are no carved decorations at all. The piers are rectangular, their capitals indicated only by simple mouldings, and the arches they carry are kept simple and unelaborated. While the treatment of the four-storey elevation of the courtyard as tier upon tier of arches that continue around all four sides of the rectangular space is unlike any to be found in other Venetian palaces, in some important ways it is also very familiar as the manifestation of a characteristic Venetian preference for arcaded screens. The garden staircase of the Palazzo Minelli is an equally clear indication of this preference, although its effect is different. The courtyard of the Fondaco dei Tedeschi is also in some respects a miniature and much more regular version of the Piazza San Marco. The rhythm of the Fondaco courtyard arches, with a wide arch on the ground level and two arches over it in the upper levels, is taken over from the old form of the Procuratie Vecchie (Plate 94).

Plate 101
FONDACO DEI TEDESCHI
Façade, 1505–6

As it stands now the Fondaco dei Tedeschi is very different from the way it appeared when it had just been completed, for the exterior was originally covered with frescoes by Giorgione and Titian. The building is rather boring without its original decoration; its architectural character alone is insufficient to make it a compelling work. The rhythm of the window placement is extremely unusual for Venice, and results from the disposition of rooms on the interior. The Fondaco was primarily an office building, and each room had on its exterior wall a fireplace flanked by windows.

The five large ground-storey arches on the canal, which provided loading space for merchandise, are framed by two block-like elements. These were once taller, projecting above the present uniform roof-line. This arrangement preserved a very old Venetian palace type which had two towers flanking a central section with an arcade on the ground floor. The placement of the *piano nobile* balcony only on the corners of the building and not across the centre has the effect of distinguishing the 'towers' from the central section, as does the slight projection of the cornices on all three levels. While the idea of an extensively painted exterior is not Venetian, the general organization of elements at the Fondaco suggests that it was influenced by someone who knew how Venetian buildings were traditionally arranged. This was probably Scarpagnino, who executed the Fondaco. While the Venetians might have decided on a painted exterior for political considerations (as long as it was painted by two of the best Venetian painters) and as an economizing measure, they seem to have cared that the building type was not completely foreign.

Plate 102 (*overleaf*)
PALAZZO DEI CAMERLENGHI
1523–5. Guglielmo dei Grigi (known as Guglielmo Bergamasco)

The building which housed the *camerlenghi* (chamberlains), magistrates with responsibility for the state treasury, was one of the few at Rialto to survive the 1514 fire. In 1523, after the reconstruction of the Fabbriche Vecchie, new quarters for the *camerlenghi* were begun. The palace carries an inscription with the date 1525, by which time it appears to have been complete.

The building is unusual in that it is free-standing and decorated equally on all sides. The façades at the base of the bridge and on the canal are framed by pairs of pilasters which flank the end windows. Each of the three entablatures breaks forward over each of the pilasters below them. A similar treatment is found at the Palazzo Grimani a San Polo (Plate 69). The exterior decoration of the Palazzo dei Camerlenghi indicates clearly that conditions had improved substantially since the fire. The friezes on all three storeys are extensively carved with garlands and roundels.

In its style the palace is quite conservative. The decorative forms are standard; there is nothing either adventurous or innovative in their combination. The building derives from such works as the east-wing courtyard façade of the Palazzo Ducale (Plate 90), designed nearly forty years earlier. This conservatism is characteristic of the 1520s, and is seen in churches of that decade as well.

The Palazzo dei Camerlenghi was the last civic work built in the 'Lombard' style. In the next decade Sansovino's Classical style for civic buildings (Plates 98, 99) would change the course of Venetian architecture.

Plate 103
RIALTO
Fabbriche Vecchie, 1514–23. Antonio Scarpagnino

After the devastating Rialto fire of January 1514, several architects submitted designs for the reconstruction of the area. Among them was Fra Giocondo of Verona, whose elaborate plan Vasari described in his *Lives*. For Fra Giocondo the fire was a blessing in disguise, offering an opportunity to rebuild the entire Rialto area on a grand and lavish scale. He envisioned a very large square area surrounded by canals (one of which would have had to be dug new), with arcades, shops, open squares, a parish church, special areas for merchants of one kind of cloth or another and sumptuous decoration. This scheme would have required the drastic enlargement of the Rialto area, the razing of many houses and two parish churches, and would have caused the destruction of more buildings than the fire had.

In 1514 the Venetians were at war with the League of Cambrai. They were short of funds, and in a hurry to rebuild the commercial centre of the city and get back to business. Fra Giocondo's expensive and long-term project was rejected in favour of a much more economical one by Scarpagnino.

The reconstructed market buildings, called the Fabbriche Vecchie, are a sparer version of the Procuratie Vecchie, with a ground-floor arcade and two storeys above. The lower level was rented out to shopkeepers, and there were offices in the upper storeys. The architecture is extremely plain. The ground-floor arches are supported by square piers with no carved capitals, and in the storeys above, the walls are stuccoed and the window frames as unadorned and inexpensive as they can be. In some of its details the Fabbriche Vecchie are quite similar to the house seen in Plate 62.

One part of Fra Giocondo's plan was eventually carried out: Vasari reports that the project called for the rebuilding of Rialto bridge in stone with shops lining both sides, and this took place in the late 1580s.

Bibliography

Ackerman, J. S., 'Architectural Practice in the Italian Renaissance', *Journal of the Society of Architectural Historians*, XIII, 1954, pp. 3–11. (Reprinted in *Renaissance Art*, ed. Creighton Gilbert, New York 1970, pp. 148–71.)

– 'L' architettura religiosa veneta in rapporto a quella toscana del rinascimento', *Bollettino del Centro di Studi di Architettura 'Andrea Palladio'*, XIX, 1977, pp. 135–64.

Angelini, L., *Bartolomeo Bono e Guglielmo d'Alzano, architetti bergamaschi in Venezia*, Bergamo 1961.

– *Le opere in Venezia di Mauro Codussi*, Milan 1945.

Bandelloni, E., 'Pietro Lombardo architetto nella critica d'arte', *Bollettino del Museo Civico di Padova*, LI, 1962, pp. 25–56.

Bassi, E., *Palazzi di Venezia*, Venice 1976.

Beltrami, L., *La 'Cà del Duca' sul Canal Grande ed altre reminiscenze sforzesche in Venezia*, Milan 1900.

– *La 'Cà del Duca' sul Canal Grande ed altre reminiscenze sforzesche in Venezia*, Milan 1906.

Chambers, D. S., *The Imperial Age of Venice: 1380–1580*, London 1970.

Cicognara, L., A. Diedo and G. A. Selva, *Le fabbriche più cospicue di Venezia*, 2 v., Venice 1815 & 1820.

De Angelis D'Ossat, G., 'Venezia e l'architettura del primo rinascimento', in *Umanesimo Europeo e Umanesimo Veneziano*, Florence 1963, pp. 435–50.

Dellwing, H., 'Die Kirchen San Zaccaria in Venedig', *Zeitschrift für Kunstgeschichte*, XXXVII, 1974, pp. 224–34.

Fontana, G., *Venezia monumentale: I Palazzi*, ed. L. Moretti, Venice 1967.

Franzoi, U., and D. di Stefano, *Le chiese di Venezia*, Venice 1976.

Gallo, R., 'L'architettura di transizione dal gotico al rinascimento e Bartolomeo Bon', *Atti dell'Istituto Veneto di Scienze, Lettere, ed Arti*, CXX, 1961/2, pp. 187–204.

Honour, H., *The Companion Guide to Venice*, London and New York 1966.

Howard, D., *Jacopo Sansovino: Architecture and Patronage in Renaissance Venice*, New Haven and London 1975.

Lane, F., *Venice, A Maritime Republic*, Baltimore and London 1975.

Lauritzen, P. and A. Zielcke, *Palaces of Venice*, Oxford 1978.

Lieberman, R., 'Venetian Church Architecture around 1500', *Bollettino del Centro Internazionale di Studi di Architettura 'Andrea Palladio'*, XIX, 1977, pp. 35–48.

– review of Puppi, L., and L. O. Puppi, 'Mauro Codussi', in *Journal of the Society of Architectural Historians*, XXXVIII, 1979, pp. 387–90.

Lorenzetti, G., *Venice and Its Lagoon*, Rome 1961.

Lorenzi, G., *Monumenti per servire alla storia del Palazzo Ducale di Venezia*, Venice 1868.

Lotz, W., 'The Roman Legacy in Jacopo Sansovino's Venetian Buildings', *Journal of the Society of Architectural Historians*, XXII, 1963, pp. 3–12. (Reprinted, with postscript, in W. Lotz, *Studies in Italian Renaissance Architecture*, Cambridge, Mass. and London 1977, pp. 140–51.)

Marx, B., 'Venezia – altera Roma! Ipotesi sull'umanesimo Veneziano', *Centro Tedesco di Studi Veneziani, Quaderni*, 10, Venice 1978.

McAndrew, J., *Venetian Architecture of the Early Renaissance*, Cambridge, Mass. 1980.

Muir, E., 'Images of Power: Art and Pageantry in Renaissance Venice', *American Historical Review*, LXXXIV, 1979, pp. 16–52.

Muraro, M., 'The Political Interpretation of Giorgione's Frescoes on the Fondaco dei Tedeschi', *Gazette des Beaux-Arts*, LXXXVI, 1975, pp. 177–83.

Paoletti, P., *L'architettura e la scultura del rinascimento in Venezia*, Venice 1893.

– *La Scuola Grande di San Marco*, Venice 1929.

Pincus, D., *The Arco Foscari: The Building of a Triumphal Gateway in Fifteenth Century Venice*, New York and London 1976.

Pullan, B., *Rich and Poor in Renaissance Venice*, Oxford 1971.

Puppi, L. and L. O. Puppi, *Mauro Codussi*, Milan 1977.

Ruskin, J., *The Stones of Venice*, 3 v., London 1851–8.

Sansovino, F., *Venetia città nobilissima et singolare, con le aggiunte di G. Martinioni*, Venice 1663. (Reprint, with analytic index by L. Moretti, Venice 1968.)

Sohm, P., 'The Staircases of the Venetian Scuole Grandi and Mauro Codussi', *Architectura*, VIII, 1978, pp. 125–49.

Spencer, J., 'The Cà del Duca in Venice and Benedetto Ferrini', *Journal of the Society of Architectural Historians*, XXIX, 1970, pp. 3–8.

Tafuri, M., *Jacopo Sansovino e l'architettura del 1500 a Venezia*, Padova 1969.

Tassini, G., *Curiosità veneziane, ovvero origini delle denominazioni stradali*, 4th edn, Venice 1886. (Reprint, with introduction by L. Moretti, Venice 1964.)

Temanza, T., *Vite dei più celebri architetti e scultori veneziani che fiorirono nel secolo decimosesto*, Venice 1778. (Reprint, with introduction and analytic index by L. Grassi, Milan 1966.)

Timofiewitsch, W., 'Genesi e struttura della chiesa del rinascimento veneziano', *Bollettino del Centro Internazionale di Studi di Architettura 'Andrea Palladio'*, VI, 1964, pp. 271–82.

Trincanato, E., *Venezia minore*, Milan 1948.

Wolters, W., *La Scultura veneziana gotica*, 2 v., Venice 1976.

Zorzi, Alvise, *Venezia scomparsa*, 2 v., 2nd edn, Milan 1977.

Index

Page numbers are in roman type. Figures are specifically so designated. All other references are to plate numbers: in **bold** type for main entries, in *italic* type for subsidiary references.

All buildings referred to are in Venice unless otherwise indicated.